By MAYA ANGELOU

MAYA ANGELOU: THE COMPLETE POETRY

MAYA ANGELOU:

The

COMPLETE POETRY

RANDOM HOUSE

New York

Published in the United States by Random House, an imprint and
division of Penguin Random House LLC, New York.

RANDOM HOUSE and the HOUSE colophon are
registered trademarks of Penguin Random House LLC.

LIBRARY OF CONGRESS CATALOGING-IN-PUBLICATION DATA
Angelou, Maya.
[Poems]
The complete poetry / Maya Angelou.
pages cm
ISBN 978-0-8129-9787-3
eBook ISBN 978-0-8129-9788-0
I. Title.
PS3551.N464 2015
811'.54—dc23
2014043508

Printed in the United States of America on acid-free paper

www.atrandom.com

2 4 6 8 9 7 5 3 1

FIRST EDITION

Title-page photograph © 1974 by Magnum Photos/Wayne Miller

Book design by Barbara M. Bachman

THIS BOOK IS
DEDICATED TO
THE GREAT LOVE
OF MY LIFE.

CONTENTS

AND STILL I RISE · 115

I SHALL NOT BE MOVED · 213

JUST GIVE ME

A COOL DRINK

OF WATER

'FORE I DIIIE

TO AMBER SAM

and

THE ZORRO MAN

PART ONE

—

WHERE LOVE IS A SCREAM OF ANGUISH

They Went Home

They went home and told their wives,
    that never once in all their lives,
    had they known a girl like me,
But . . . They went home.

They said my house was licking clean,
    no word I spoke was ever mean,
    I had an air of mystery,
But . . . They went home.

My praises were on all men's lips,
    they liked my smile, my wit, my hips,
    they'd spend one night, or two or three.
But . . .

The Gamut

Soft you day, be velvet soft,
    My true love approaches,
Look you bright, you dusty sun,
    Array your golden coaches.

    Soft you wind, be soft as silk,
My true love is speaking.
    Hold you birds, your silver throats,
His golden voice I'm seeking.

Come you death, in haste, do come,
    My shroud of black be weaving,
Quiet my heart, be deathly quiet,
    My true love is leaving.

A Zorro Man

Here
in the wombed room
silk purple drapes
flash a light as subtle
as your hands before
love-making

Here
in the covered lens
I catch a
clitoral image of
your general inhabitation
long and like a
late dawn in winter

Here
this clean mirror
traps me unwilling
in a gone time
when I was love
and you were booted and brave
and trembling for me.

To a Man

My man is
Black Golden Amber
Changing.
Warm mouths of Brandy Fine
Cautious sunlight on a patterned rug
Coughing laughter, rocked on a whorl of French tobacco
Graceful turns on woolen stilts
Secretive?
A cat's eye.
Southern. Plump and tender with navy-bean sullenness
And did I say "Tender"?
The gentleness
A big cat stalks through stubborn bush
And did I mention "Amber"?
The heatless fire consuming itself.
Again. Anew. Into ever neverlessness.
My man is Amber
Changing
Always into itself
New. Now New.
Still itself.
Still.

Late October

Carefully
the leaves of autumn
sprinkle down the tinny
sound of little dyings
and skies sated
of ruddy sunsets
of roseate dawns
roil ceaselessly in
cobweb greys and turn
to black
for comfort.

Only lovers
see the fall
a signal end to endings
a gruffish gesture alerting
those who will not be alarmed
that we begin to stop
in order simply
to begin
again.

No Loser, No Weeper

"I hate to lose something,"
    then she bent her head,
"even a dime, I wish I was dead.
I can't explain it. No more to be said.
'Cept I hate to lose something.

"I lost a doll once and cried for a week.
She could open her eyes, and do all but speak.
I believe she was took, by some doll-snatching sneak.
I tell you, I hate to lose something.

"A watch of mine once, got up and walked away.
It had twelve numbers on it and for the time of day.
I'll never forget it and all I can say
Is I really hate to lose something.

"Now if I felt that way 'bout a watch and a toy,
What you think I feel 'bout my lover-boy?
I ain't threatening you, madam, but he is my evening's joy.
And I mean I really hate to lose something."

When You Come to Me

When you come to me, unbidden,
Beckoning me
    To long-ago rooms,
Where memories lie.

Offering me, as to a child, an attic,
Gatherings of days too few,
    Baubles of stolen kisses,
Trinkets of borrowed loves,
    Trunks of secret words,

I CRY.

Remembering

Soft grey ghosts crawl up my sleeve
to peer into my eyes
while I within deny their threats
and answer them with lies.

Mushlike memories perform
a ritual on my lips
I lie in stolid hopelessness
and they lay my soul in strips.

In a Time

In a time of secret wooing
Today prepares tomorrow's ruin
Left knows not what right is doing
My heart is torn asunder.

In a time of furtive sighs
Sweet hellos and sad goodbyes
Half-truths told and entire lies
My conscience echoes thunder.

In a time when kingdoms come
Joy is brief as summer's fun
Happiness its race has run
Then pain stalks in to plunder.

Tears

Tears
The crystal rags
Viscous tatters
of a worn-through soul.

Moans
Deep swan song
Blue farewell
of a dying dream.

The Detached

We die,
Welcoming Bluebeards to our darkening closets,
Stranglers to our outstretched necks,
       Stranglers, who neither care nor
       care to know that
       DEATH IS INTERNAL.

We pray,
Savoring sweet the teethed lies,
Bellying the grounds before alien gods,
       Gods, who neither know nor
       wish to know that
       HELL IS INTERNAL.

We love,
Rubbing the nakednesses with gloved hands,
Inverting our mouths in tongued kisses,
       Kisses that neither touch nor
       care to touch if
       LOVE IS INTERNAL.

To a Husband

Your voice at times a fist
    Tight in your throat
Jabs ceaselessly at phantoms
    In the room,
Your hand a carved and
    Skimming boat
Goes down the Nile
    To point out Pharaoh's tomb.

You're Africa to me
    At brightest dawn.
The Congo's green and
    Copper's brackish hue,
A continent to build
    With Black Man's brawn.
I sit at home and see it all
    Through you.

Accident

Tonight
    when you spread your pallet
of magic,
    I escaped.
Sitting apart,
    I saw you grim and unkempt.
Your vulgarness
    not of living,
your demands
    not from need.

Tonight
    as you sprinkled your brain-dust
of rainbows,
    I had no eyes.
Seeing all
I saw the colors fade
and change.
    The blood, red dulled
through the dyes,
and the naked
Black-White truth.

Let's Majeste

I sit a throne upon the times
when Kings are rare and
Consorts
slide into the grease of scullery maids.

So gaily wave a crown of light
(astride the royal chair) that blinds
the commoners who genuflect and cross their fingers.

The years will lie beside me
on the queenly bed.
And coupled we'll await
the ages' dust to cake my lids again.

And when the rousing kiss is given,
why must it always be a fairy, and
only just a Prince?

After

No sound falls
from the moaning sky
No scowl wrinkles
the evening pool
    The stars lean down
    A stony brilliance
    While birds fly.

The market leers
its empty shelves
Streets bare bosoms
to scanty cars
    This bed yawns
    beneath the weight
    of our absent selves.

The Mothering Blackness

She came home running
    back to the mothering blackness
    deep in the smothering blackness
white tears icicle gold plains of her face
    She came home running

She came down creeping
    here to the black arms waiting
    now to the warm heart waiting
rime of alien dreams befrosts her rich brown face
    She came down creeping

She came home blameless
    black yet as Hagar's daughter
    tall as was Sheba's daughter
threats of northern winds die on the desert's face
    She came home blameless

On Diverse Deviations

When love is a shimmering curtain
Before a door of chance
That leads to a world in question
Wherein the macabrous dance
Of bones that rattle in silence
Of blinded eyes and rolls
Of thick lips thin, denying
A thousand powdered moles,
Where touch to touch is feel
And life a weary whore
    I would be carried off, not gently
    To a shore,
    Where love is the scream of anguish
    And no curtain drapes the door.

Mourning Grace

If today I follow death,
go down its trackless wastes,
salt my tongue on hardened tears
for my precious dear time's waste
race
along that promised cave in a headlong
deadlong
haste,
Will you
have
the
grace
to mourn for
me?

How I Can Lie to You

now thread my voice
with lies
of lightness
force within
my mirror eyes
the cold disguise
of sad and wise
decisions.

Sounds Like Pearls

Sounds
    Like pearls
Roll off your tongue
    To grace this eager ebon ear.

Doubt and fear,
    Ungainly things,
With blushings
    Disappear.

PART TWO

JUST BEFORE THE WORLD ENDS

When I Think About Myself

When I think about myself,
I almost laugh myself to death,
My life has been one great big joke,
A dance that's walked,
A song that's spoke,
I laugh so hard I almost choke,
When I think about myself.

Sixty years in these folks' world,
The child I works for calls me girl,
I say "Yes ma'am" for working's sake.
Too proud to bend,
Too poor to break,
I laugh until my stomach ache,
When I think about myself.

My folks can make me split my side,
I laughed so hard I nearly died,
The tales they tell sound just like lying,
They grow the fruit,
But eat the rind,
I laugh until I start to crying,
When I think about my folks.

On a Bright Day, Next Week

On a bright day, next week
Just before the bomb falls
Just before the world ends
   Just before I die

All my tears will powder
Black in dust like ashes
Black like Buddha's belly
   Black and hot and dry

Then will mercy tumble
Falling down in godheads
Falling on the children
   Falling from the sky

Letter to an Aspiring Junkie

Let me hip you to the streets,
Jim,
Ain't nothing happening.
Maybe some tomorrows gone up in smoke,
raggedy preachers, telling a joke
to lonely, son-less old ladies' maids.

Nothing happening,
Nothing shakin', Jim.
A slough of young cats riding that
cold, white horse,
a grey old monkey on their back, of course,
does rodeo tricks.

No haps, man.
No haps.
A worn-out pimp, with a space-age conk,
setting up some fool for a game of tonk,
or poker or
get 'em dead and alive.

The streets?
Climb into the streets, man, like you climb
into the ass end of a lion.
Then it's fine.
It's a bug-a-loo and a shing-a-ling,
African dreams on a buck-and-a-wing and a prayer.
That's the streets, man,
Nothing happening.

Miss Scarlett, Mr. Rhett and Other Latter-Day Saints

Novitiates sing Ave
Before the whipping posts,
Crisscrossing their breasts and
tearstained robes
in the yielding dark.

Animated by the human sacrifice
(Golgotha in blackface)
Priests glow purely white on the
bas-relief of a plantation shrine.

(O Sing)
You are gone but not forgotten.
Hail, Scarlett. Requiescat in pace.

God-Makers smear brushes in
blood/gall
to etch frescoes on your
ceilinged tomb.

(O Sing)
Hosanna, King Kotton.

Shadowed couplings of infidels
tempt stigmata from the nipples
of your true believers.

(Chant Maternoster)
Hallowed Little Eva.

Ministers make novena with the
charred bones of four
very small
very black
very young children

(Intone D I X I E)

And guard the relics
of your intact hymen,
daily putting to death,
into eternity,
The stud, his seed,
His seed
His seed.

(O Sing)
Hallelujah, pure Scarlett,
Blessed Rhett, the Martyr.

Times-Square-Shoeshine-Composition

I'm the best that ever done it
(pow pow)
  That's my title and I won it
  (pow pow)
I ain't lying, I'm the best
(pow pow)
  Come and put me to the test
  (pow pow)

I'll clean 'em till they squeak
(pow pow)
  In the middle of next week
  (pow pow)
I'll shine 'em till they whine
(pow pow)
  Till they call me master mine
  (pow pow)

For a quarter and a dime
(pow pow)
  You can get the dee-luxe shine
  (pow pow)
Say you wanta pay a quarter?
(pow pow)
  Then you give that to your daughter
  (pow pow)

I ain't playing dozens, mister
(pow pow)
  You can give it to your sister
  (pow pow)

Any way you want to read it
(pow pow)
    Maybe it's your momma need it
    (pow pow)

Say I'm like a greedy bigot
(pow pow)
    I'm a cap'talist, can you dig it?
    (pow pow)

Faces

Faces and more remember
then reject
the brown caramel days of youth.
Reject the sun-sucked tit of
childhood mornings.
Poke a muzzle of war in the trust-frozen eyes of a favored doll.
Breathe, Brother,
and displace a moment's hate with organized love.
A poet screams "CHRIST WAITS AT THE SUBWAY!"
But who sees?

To a Freedom Fighter

You drink a bitter draught.
I sip the tears your eyes fight to hold,
A cup of lees, of henbane steeped in chaff.
Your breast is hot,
Your anger black and cold,
Through evening's rest, you dream,
I hear the moans, you die a thousands' death.
When cane straps flog the body
dark and lean, you feel the blow.
I hear it in your breath.

Riot: 60's

Our
YOUR FRIEND CHARLIE pawnshop
was a glorious blaze
I heard the flames lick
then eat the trays
of zircons
mounted in red gold alloys

Easter clothes and stolen furs
burned in the attic
radios and teevees
crackled with static
plugged in
only to a racial outlet

Some
thought the FRIENDLY FINANCE FURNITURE CO.
burned higher
When a leopard-print sofa with gold legs
(which makes into a bed)
caught fire
an admiring groan from the waiting horde
"Absentee landlord
you got that shit"

Lighting: a hundred Watts
Detroit, Newark and New York
Screeching nerves, exploding minds
lives tied to a policeman's whistle
a welfare worker's doorbell
finger

Hospitality, southern-style
corn pone grits and you-all smile
whole blocks novae
brand-new stars
policemen caught in their
brand-new cars
Chugga chugga chigga
git me one nigga
lootin' n burnin'
he won't git far

Watermelons, summer ripe
grey neckbones and boiling tripe
supermarket roastin' like the
noonday sun
national guard nervous with his shiny gun
goose the motor quicker
here's my nigga picka
shoot him in the belly
shoot him while he run

We Saw Beyond Our Seeing

We saw beyond our seeming
   These days of bloodied screaming

Of children dying bloated
   Out where the lilies floated

Of men all noosed and dangling
   Within the temples strangling

Our guilt grey fungus growing
   We knew and lied our knowing

Deafened and unwilling
   We aided in the killing

And now our souls lie broken
   Dry tablets without token.

Black Ode

Your beauty is a thunder
And I am set a wandering—a wandering
Deafened
Down twilight tin-can alleys
And moist sounds
"OOo wee, Baby, look what you could get if your name
    was Willie"
Oh, to dip your words like snuff.

A laughter, black and streaming
And I am come a being—a being
Rounded
Up Baptist aisles, so moaning
And moist sounds
"Bless her heart. Take your bed and walk.
You been heavy burdened"
Oh, to lick your love like tears.

No No No No

No
the two-legg'd beasts
that walk like men
play stink finger in their crusty asses
while crackling babies
in napalm coats
stretch mouths to receive
burning tears
on splitting tongues
JUST GIVE ME A COOL DRINK OF WATER 'FORE I DIIIE

No
the gap-legg'd whore
of the eastern shore
enticing Europe to COME
in her
and turns her pigeon-shit back to me
to me
who stoked the coal that drove the ships
which brought her over the sinuous cemetery
of my many brothers

No
the cocktailed afternoons
of what can I do.
In my white layered pink world
I've let your men cram my mouth
with their black throbbing hate
and I swallowed after
I've let your mammies
steal from my kitchens
(I was always half-amused)

I've chuckled the chins of
your topsy-haired pickaninnies.
What more can I do?
I'll never be black like you.
(HALLELUJAH)

No
the red-shoed priests riding
palanquined
in barefoot children country
the plastered saints gazing down
beneficently
on kneeling mothers
picking undigested beans
from yesterday's shit.

I have waited
toes curled, hat rolled
heart and genitals
in hand
on the back porches
of forever
in the kitchens and fields
of rejections
on the cold marble steps
of America's White Out-House
in the drop seats of buses
and the open flies of war

No more
the dream that you
will cease haunting me
down in fetid swamps of fear
and will turn to embrace your own

humanity
which I AM

No more
the hope that
the razored insults
which mercury-slide over your tongue
will be forgotten
and you will learn the words of love
Mother Brother Father Sister Lover Friend

My hopes
dying slowly
rose petals falling
beneath an autumn red moon
will not adorn your unmarked graves

My dreams
lying quietly
a dark pool under the trees
will not carry your name
to a forgetful shore
And what a pity

What a pity
that pity has folded in upon itself
an old man's mouth
whose teeth are gone
and I have no pity.

My Guilt

My guilt is "slavery's chains," too long
the clang of iron falls down the years.
This brother's sold, this sister's gone,
is bitter wax, lining my ears.
My guilt made music with the tears.

My crime is "heroes, dead and gone,"
dead Vesey, Turner, Gabriel,
dead Malcolm, Marcus, Martin King.
They fought too hard, they loved too well.
My crime is I'm alive to tell.

My sin is "hanging from a tree,"
I do not scream, it makes me proud.
I take to dying like a man.
I do it to impress the crowd.
My sin lies in not screaming loud.

The Calling of Names

He went to being called a colored man
after answering to "hey, nigger."
Now that's a big jump,
anyway you figger.
        Hey, Baby, watch my smoke.
From colored man to Negro,
With the *N* in caps,
was like saying Japanese
instead of saying Japs.
        I mean, during the war.
The next big step
was a change for true,
From Negro in caps
to being a Jew.
        Now, Sing, Yiddish Mama.
Light, Yellow, Brown
and Dark-brown skin,
were okay colors to
describe him then.
        He was a Bouquet of Roses.
He changed his seasons
like an almanac.
Now you'll get hurt
if you don't call him "Black."
        Nigguh, I ain't playin' this time.

On Working White Liberals

I don't ask the Foreign Legion
Or anyone to win my freedom
Or to fight my battle better than I can,

Though there's one thing that I cry for
I believe enough to die for
That is every man's responsibility to man.

I'm afraid they'll have to prove first
That they'll watch the Black man move first
Then follow him with faith to kingdom come.
This rocky road is not paved for us,
So, I'll believe in Liberals' aid for us
When I see a white man load a Black man's gun.

Sepia Fashion Show

Their hair, pomaded, faces jaded
bones protruding, hip-wise,
the models strutted, backed and butted,
then stuck their mouths out, lip-wise.

They'd nasty manners, held like banners,
while they looked down their nose-wise.
I'd see 'em in hell, before they'd sell
me one thing they're wearing, clothes-wise.

The Black Bourgeois, who all say "yah"
when yeah is what they're meaning,
should look around, both up and down,
before they set out preening.

"Indeed," they swear, "that's what I'll wear
when I go country-clubbing."
I'd remind them please, look at those knees,
you got at Miss Ann's scrubbing.

The Thirteens (Black)

Your Momma took to shouting,
Your Poppa's gone to war,
Your sister's in the streets,
Your brother's in the bar,
The thirteens. Right On.

Your cousin's taking smack,
Your uncle's in the joint,
Your buddy's in the gutter,
Shooting for his point,
The thirteens. Right On.

And you, you make me sorry,
You out here by yourself,
I'd call you something dirty,
But there just ain't nothing left,
'cept
The thirteens. Right On.

The Thirteens (White)

Your Momma kissed the chauffeur,
Your Poppa balled the cook,
Your sister did the dirty,
in the middle of the book,
The thirteens. Right On.

Your daughter wears a jock strap,
Your son he wears a bra,
Your brother jonesed your cousin
in the back seat of the car.
The thirteens. Right On.

Your money thinks you're something,
But if I'd learned to curse,
I'd tell you what your name is,
But there just ain't nothing worse
than
The thirteens. Right On.

Harlem Hopscotch

One foot down, then hop! It's hot.
    Good things for the ones that's got.
Another jump, now to the left.
    Everybody for hisself.

In the air, now both feet down.
    Since you black, don't stick around.
Food is gone, the rent is due,
    Curse and cry and then jump two.

All the people out of work,
    Hold for three, then twist and jerk.
Cross the line, they count you out.
    That's what hopping's all about.

Both feet flat, the game is done.
They think I lost. I think I won.

OH PRAY

MY WINGS ARE

GONNA FIT

ME WELL

TO

PAUL

PART ONE

Pickin Em Up
and Layin Em Down

There's a long-legged girl
in San Francisco
by the Golden Gate.
She said she'd give me all I wanted
but I just couldn't wait.
I started to
Pickin em up
          and layin em down,
Pickin em up
          and layin em down,
Pickin em up
          and layin em down,
gettin to the next town
Baby.

There's a pretty brown
in Birmingham.
Boys, she little and cute
but when she like to tied me down
I had to grab my suit and started to
Pickin em up
          and layin em down,
Pickin em up
          and layin em down,
Pickin em up
          and layin em down,
gettin to the next town
Baby.

I met that lovely Detroit lady
and thought my time had come

But just before I said "I do"
I said "I got to run" and started to
Pickin em up
             and layin em down,
Pickin em up
             and layin em down,
Pickin em up
             and layin em down,
gettin to the next town
Baby.

There ain't no words for what I feel
about a pretty face
But if I stay I just might miss
a prettier one some place
I started to
Pickin em up
             and layin em down,
Pickin em up
             and layin em down,
Pickin em up
             and layin em down,
gettin to the next town
Baby.

Here's to Adhering

I went to a party
   out in Hollywood,
The atmosphere was shoddy
   but the drinks were good,
      and that's where I heard you laugh.

I then went cruising
   on an old Greek ship,
The crew was amusing
   but the guests weren't hip,
      that's where I found your hands.

On to the Sahara
   in a caravan,
The sun struck like an arrow
   but the nights were grand,
      and that's how I found your chest.

An evening in the Congo
   where the Congo ends,
I found myself alone, oh
   but I made some friends,
      that's where I saw your face.

I have been devoting
   all my time to get
Parts of you out floating
   still unglued as yet.

Won't you pull yourself together

For

    Me

   O N C E

On Reaching Forty

Other acquainted years
sidle
with modest
decorum
across the scrim of toughened
tears and to a stage
planked with laughter boards
and waxed with rueful loss.
But forty
with the authorized
brazenness of a uniformed
cop stomps
no-knocking
into the script
bumps a funky grind on the
shabby curtain of youth
and delays the action.

Unless you have the inborn
wisdom
and grace
and are clever enough
to die at
thirty-nine.

The Telephone

It comes in black
and blue, indecisive
beige. In red and chaperons my life.
Sitting like a strict
and spinstered aunt
spiked between my needs
and need.

It tats the day, crocheting
other people's lives
in neat arrangements,
ignoring me,
busy with the hemming
of strangers' overlong affairs or
the darning of my
neighbors' worn-out
dreams.

From Monday, the morning of the week,
through mid-times
noon and Sunday's dying
light. It sits silent.
Its needle sound
does not transfix my ear
or draw my longing to
a close.

Ring. Damn you!

PART TWO

Passing Time

Your skin like dawn
Mine like dusk.

One paints the beginning
of a certain end.

The other, the end of a
sure beginning.

Now Long Ago

One innocent spring
your voice meant to me
less than tires turning
on a distant street.

Your name, perhaps spoken,
led no chorus of
batons
unrehearsed
to crush against my
empty chest.

That cool spring
was shortened by
your summer, bold, impatient
and all forgotten
except when silence
turns the key
into my midnight bedroom
and comes to sleep upon your
pillow.

Greyday

The day hangs heavy
loose and grey
when you're away.

A crown of thorns
a shirt of hair
is what I wear.

No one knows
my lonely heart
when we're apart.

Poor Girl

You've got another love
    and I know it
Someone who adores you
    just like me
Hanging on your words
    like they were gold
Thinking that she understands
    your soul
Poor Girl
      Just like me.

You're breaking another heart
    and I know it
And there's nothing
    I can do
If I try to tell her
    what I know
She'll misunderstand
    and make me go
Poor Girl
      Just like me.

You're going to leave her too
    and I know it
She'll never know
    what made you go
She'll cry and wonder
    what went wrong
Then she'll begin
    to sing this song
Poor Girl
      Just like me.

Come. And Be My Baby

The highway is full of big cars
going nowhere fast
And folks is smoking anything that'll burn
Some people wrap their lives around a cocktail glass
And you sit wondering
where you're going to turn.
I got it.
Come. And be my baby.

Some prophets say the world is gonna end tomorrow
But others say we've got a week or two
The paper is full of every kind of blooming horror
And you sit wondering
What you're gonna do.
I got it.
Come. And be my baby.

Senses of Insecurity

I couldn't tell fact from fiction
    or if my dream was true,
The only sure prediction
    in this whole world was you.
I'd touched your features inchly,
    heard love and dared the cost.
The scented spiel reeled me unreal
    and found my senses lost.

Alone

Lying, thinking
Last night
How to find my soul a home
Where water is not thirsty
And bread loaf is not stone
I came up with one thing
And I don't believe I'm wrong
That nobody,
But nobody
Can make it out here alone.

Alone, all alone
Nobody, but nobody
Can make it out here alone.

There are some millionaires
With money they can't use
Their wives run round like banshees
Their children sing the blues
They've got expensive doctors
To cure their hearts of stone.
But nobody
No, nobody
Can make it out here alone.

Alone, all alone
Nobody, but nobody
Can make it out here alone.

Now if you listen closely
I'll tell you what I know
Storm clouds are gathering

The wind is gonna blow
The race of man is suffering
And I can hear the moan,
'Cause nobody,
But nobody
Can make it out here alone.

Alone, all alone
Nobody, but nobody
Can make it out here alone.

Communication I

She wished of him a lover's kiss and
nights of coupled twining.
They laced themselves
between the trees
and to the water's edge.

Reminding her
the cratered moon lay light-years away,
he spoke of Greece, the Parthenon
and Cleopatra's barge.

She splayed her foot
up to the shin
within the ocean brine.

He quoted Pope and Bernard Shaw
and *Catcher in the Rye.*

Her sandal lost,
she dried her toe
and then she mopped her brow.

Dry-eyed
she walked into her room
and frankly told her mother,
"Of all he said, I understood
he said he loved another."

Communication II

FOR ADELE

The Student

The dust of ancient pages
had never touched his face,
and fountains black and comely
were mummied in a place
beyond
his young un-knowing.

The Teacher

She shared the lettered strivings
of etched Pharaonic walls
and Reconstruction's anguish
resounded down the halls
of all her
dry dreams.

Wonder

A day
drunk with the nectar of
nowness
weaves its way between
the years
to find itself at the flophouse
of night
to sleep and be seen
no more.

Will I be less
dead because I wrote this
poem or you more because
you read it
long years hence.

A Conceit

Give me your hand.

Make room for me
to lead and follow
you
beyond this rage of poetry.

Let others have
the privacy of
touching words
and love of loss
of love.

For me
Give me your hand.

PART THREE

Request

If this country is a bastard
will the lowdown mother user
who ran off
and left the woman
moaning in her
green delivery
please come back and claim
his love child.
Give a legal name to beg from
for the first
time of its life.

Africa

Thus she had lain
sugarcane sweet
deserts her hair
golden her feet
mountains her breasts
two Niles her tears.
Thus she has lain
Black through the years.

Over the white seas
rime white and cold
brigands ungentled
icicle bold
took her young daughters
sold her strong sons
churched her with Jesus
bled her with guns.
Thus she has lain.

Now she is rising
remember her pain
remember the losses
her screams loud and vain
remember her riches
her history slain
now she is striding
although she had lain.

America

The gold of her promise
    has never been mined

Her borders of justice
    not clearly defined

Her crops of abundance
    the fruit and the grain

Have not fed the hungry
    nor eased that deep pain

Her proud declarations
    are leaves on the wind

Her southern exposure
    black death did befriend

Discover this country
    dead centuries cry

Erect noble tablets
    where none can decry

"She kills her bright future
    and rapes for a sou

Then entraps her children
    with legends untrue"

I beg you

Discover this country.

For Us, Who Dare Not Dare

Be me a Pharaoh
Build me high pyramids of stone and question
See me the Nile
at twilight
and jaguars moving to
the slow cool draught.

Swim me Congo
Hear me the tails of alligators
flapping waves that reach
a yester shore.

Swing me vines, beyond that baobab tree,
and talk me chief
Sing me birds
flash color lightening through bright green leaves.

Taste me fruit
its juice free-falling from
a mother tree.

Know me

Africa.

Lord, in My Heart

FOR COUNTEE CULLEN

Holy haloes
    Ring me round

Spirit waves on
    Spirit sound

Meshach and
    Abednego

Golden chariot
    Swinging low

I recite them
    in my sleep

Jordan's cold
    and briny deep

Bible lessons
    Sunday school

Bow before the
    Golden Rule

Now I wonder
    If I tried

Could I turn my
    cheek aside

Marvelling with
    afterthought

Let the blow fall
    saying naught

Of my true Christ-
    like control

And the nature
    of my soul

Would I strike with
    rage divine

Till the culprit
    fell supine

Hit out broad all
    fury red

Till my foes are
    fallen dead

Teachers of my
    early youth

Taught forgiveness
    stressed the truth

Here then is my
    Christian lack:

If I'm struck then
    I'll strike back.

Artful Pose

Of falling leaves and melting
snows, of birds
in their delights
Some poets sing
their melodies
tendering my nights
sweetly.

My pencil halts
and will not go
along that quiet path.
I need to write
of lovers false

and hate
and hateful wrath
quickly.

PART FOUR

The Couple

Discard the fear and what
was she?   Of rag and bones
a mimicry of woman's
fairy-ness
Archaic at its birth.

Discharge the hate and when
was he?   Disheveled moans
a mimesis of man's
estate
deceited for its worth.

Dissolve the greed and why
were they?   Enfeebled thrones
a memory of mortal
kindliness
exiled from this earth.

The Pusher

He bad
O he bad
He make a honky
poot. Make a honky's
blue eyes squint
anus tight, when
my man look in
the light blue eyes.

He thinks
He don't play
His Afro crown raises
eyes. Raises eyebrows
of wonder and dark
envy when he, combed
out, hits the street.

He sleek
Dashiki
Wax-printed on his skin
remembrances of Congo dawns
laced across his chest.
Red Blood Red and Black.

He bought
O he got
Malcolm's paper
back. Checked out the
photo, caught a few godly
lines. Then wondered how
many wives/daughters of
Honky (miscalled The Man)
bird snake

caught, dug them both.
(Him, Fro-ed Dashiki-ed
and the book.)

He stashed
He stands stashed
Near, too near the MLK
Library. P.S. naught
naught naught. Breathing
slaughter on the Malcolm X
Institute. Whole fist
balled, fingers pressing
palm. Shooting up through
Honky's blue-eyed sky.

"BLACK IS!"
"NATION TIME!"
"TOMORROW'S GLORY HERE TODAY"

Pry free the hand
Observe our Black present.
There lie soft on that
copper palm, a death of
coke. A kill of horse
eternal night's barbiturates.
One hundred youths
sped down to
Speed.

He right
O he bad
He badder than death
yet gives no sweet
release.

Chicken-Licken

She was afraid of men,
sin and the humors
of the night.
When she saw a bed
locks clicked
in her brain.

She screwed a frown
around and plugged
it in the keyhole.
Put a chain across
her door and closed
her mind.

Her bones were found
round thirty years later
when they razed
her building to
put up a parking lot.

Autopsy read:
dead of acute peoplelessness.

PART FIVE

I Almost Remember

I almost remember
    smiling some
years past
    even combing the ceiling
with the teeth of a laugh
(longer ago than the
      smile).
Open night news-eyed I watch
channels of hunger
    written on children's faces
    bursting bellies balloon
in the air of my day room.

There was a smile, I recall
now jelled in
a never yester glow. Even a laugh
that tickled the tits of
heaven
(older than the smile).
In graphs, afraid, I see the black
brown hands and
white thin yellowed fingers

Slip slipping from the
ledge of life. Forgotten by
all but hatred.
Ignored
by all but disdain.

On late evenings when
quiet inhabits my garden
when grass sleeps and

streets are only paths for silent
mist

I seem to remember

Smiling.

Prisoner

Even sunlight dares
and trembles through
my bars
to shimmer
dances on
the floor.
A clang of
lock and
keys and heels
and blood-dried
guns.
Even sunshine
dares.

It's jail
    and bail
then rails to run.

Guard grey men
serve plates of rattle
noise and concrete
death and beans.
Then pale sun stumbles
through the poles of
iron to warm the horror
of grey guard men.

It's jail
    and bail
then rails to run.

Black night. The me
myself of me sleeks
in the folds and history
of fear. To secret hold
me deep and close my
ears of lulls and clangs
and memory of hate.
Then night and sleep
and dreams.

It's jail
        and bail
then rails to run.

Woman Me

Your smile, delicate
rumor of peace.
Deafening revolutions nestle in the
cleavage of
your breasts.
Beggar-Kings and red-ringed Priests
seek glory at the meeting
of your thighs.
A grasp of Lions. A lap of Lambs.

Your tears, jeweled
strewn a diadem
caused Pharaohs to ride
deep in the bosom of the
Nile. Southern spas lash fast
their doors upon the night when
winds of death blow down your name
A bride of hurricanes.   A swarm of summer wind.

Your laughter, pealing tall
above the bells of ruined cathedrals.
Children reach between your teeth
for charts to live their lives.
A stomp of feet. A bevy of swift hands.

John J.

His soul curdled
standing milk
      childhood's right gone wrong.

Plum-blue skin brown dusted
eyes black shining.
      (His momma didn't want him.)

The round head slick silk
Turn-around, fall-down curls.
Old ladies smelling of flour
and talcum powder, Cashmere Bouquet, said
"This child is pretty enough to be a girl."
      (But his momma didn't want him.)

John J. grinned a "How can you resist me?"
and danced to conjure lightning from
a morning's summer sky.
Gave the teacher an apple kiss.
      (But his momma didn't want him.)

His nerves stretched two thousand miles
found a flinging singing lady,
breasting a bar
calling straights on the dice,
gin over ice,
and the 30's version of
everybody in the
pool.
      (She didn't want him.)

Southeast Arkanasia

After Eli Whitney's gin
brought to generations' end
bartered flesh and broken bones
Did it cleanse you of your sin
      Did you ponder?

Now, when farmers bury wheat
and the cow men dump the sweet
butter down on Davy Jones
Does it sanctify your street
        Do you wonder?

Or is guilt your nightly mare
bucking wake your evenings' share
of the stilled repair of groans
and the absence of despair
          over yonder?

Song for the Old Ones

My Fathers sit on benches
    their flesh counts every plank
    the slats leave dents of darkness
deep in their withered flanks.

They nod like broken candles
    all waxed and burnt profound
    they say "It's understanding
that makes the world go round."

There in those pleated faces
    I see the auction block
    the chains and slavery's coffles
the whip and lash and stock.

My Fathers speak in voices
    that shred my fact and sound
    they say "It's our submission
that makes the world go round."

They used the finest cunning
    their naked wits and wiles
    the lowly Uncle Tomming
and Aunt Jemimas' smiles.

They've laughed to shield their crying
    then shuffled through their dreams
    and stepped 'n' fetched a country
to write the blues with screams.

I understand their meaning
    it could and did derive
    from living on the edge of death
They kept my race alive.

Child Dead in Old Seas

Father,
I wait for you in oceans
tides washing pyramids high
above my head.
Waves, undulating
corn rows around my
black feet.
The heavens shift and
stars find holes set
new in dark infirmity.
My search goes on.
Dainty shells on ash-like wrists
of debutantes remember you.
Childhood's absence has
not stilled your
voice. My ear
listens. You whisper
on the watery passage.

Deep dirges moan
from the
belly of the sea
and your song
floats to me
of lost savannahs
green and
drums. Of palm trees bending
woman-like swaying
grape-blue children
laugh on beaches
of sand as
white as your bones

clean
on the foot of
long-ago waters.

Father.
I wait for you
wrapped in
the entrails of
whales. Your
blood now
blues
spume
over
the rippled
surface of our
grave.

Take Time Out

When you see them
on a freeway hitching rides
wearing beads
with packs by their sides
you ought to ask
What's all the
warring and the jarring
and the
killing and
the thrilling
all about.

Take Time Out.

When you see him
with a band around his head
and an army surplus bunk
that makes his bed
you'd better ask
What's all the
beating and
the cheating and
the bleeding and
the needing
all about.

Take Time Out.

When you see her walking
barefoot in the rain
and you know she's tripping

on a one-way train
you need to ask
What's all the
lying and the
dying and
the running and
the gunning
all about.

Take Time Out.

Use a minute
feel some sorrow
for the folks
who think tomorrow
is a place that they
can call up
on the phone.
Take a month
and show some kindness
for the folks
who thought that blindness
was an illness that
affected eyes alone.

If you know that youth
is dying on the run
and my daughter trades
dope stories with your son
we'd better see
what all our
fearing and our
jeering and our

crying and
our lying
brought about.

Take Time Out.

Elegy

FOR HARRIET TUBMAN & FREDRICK DOUGLASS

I lie down in my grave
and watch my children
grow
Proud blooms
above the weeds of death.

Their petals wave
and still nobody
knows the soft black
dirt that is my winding
sheet. The worms, my friends,
yet tunnel holes in
bones and through those
apertures I see the rain.
The sunfelt warmth
now jabs
within my space and
brings me roots of my
children born.

Their seeds must fall
and press beneath
this earth,
and find me where
I wait. My only need to
fertilize their birth.

I lie down in my grave
and watch my children
grow.

Reverses

How often must we
  butt to head
Mind to ass
  flank to nuts
  cock to elbow
  hip to toe
  soul to shoulder
  confront ourselves
  in our past.

Little Girl Speakings

Ain't nobody better'n my Daddy,
    you keep yo' quauter,
    I ain't yo' daughter,
Ain't nobody better'n my Daddy.

Ain't nothing prettier'n my dollie,
    heard what I said,
    don't pat her head,
Ain't nothing prettier'n my dollie.

No lady cookinger than my Mommy,
    smell that pie,
    see I don't lie,
No lady cookinger than my Mommy.

This Winter Day

The kitchen is its readiness
white green and orange things
leak their blood selves in the soup.

Ritual sacrifice that snaps
an odor at my nose and starts
my tongue to march
slipping in the liquid of its drip.

The day, silver striped
in rain, is balked against
my window and the soup.

AND STILL
I RISE

THIS BOOK IS DEDICATED

to a few

of the Good Guys

You to laugh with

You to cry to

I can just about make

it over

JESSICA MITFORD

GERARD W. PURCELL

JAY ALLEN

PART ONE

TOUCH ME, LIFE, NOT SOFTLY

A Kind of Love, Some Say

Is it true the ribs can tell
The kick of a beast from a
Lover's fist? The bruised
Bones recorded well
The sudden shock, the
Hard impact. Then swollen lids,
Sorry eyes, spoke not
Of lost romance, but hurt.

Hate often is confused. Its
Limits are in zones beyond itself. And
Sadists will not learn that
Love, by nature, exacts a pain
Unequalled on the rack.

Country Lover

Funky blues
Keen toed shoes
High water pants
Saddy night dance
Red soda water
and anybody's daughter

Remembrance

FOR PAUL

Your hands easy
weight, teasing the bees
hived in my hair, your smile at the
slope of my cheek. On the
occasion, you press
above me, glowing, spouting
readiness, mystery rapes
my reason.

When you have withdrawn
your self and the magic, when
only the smell of your
love lingers between
my breasts, then, only
then, can I greedily consume
your presence.

Where We Belong, A Duet

In every town and village,
In every city square,
In crowded places
I searched the faces
Hoping to find
Someone to care.

I read mysterious meanings
In the distant stars,
Then I went to schoolrooms
And poolrooms
And half-lighted cocktail bars.
Braving dangers,
Going with strangers,
I don't even remember their names.
I was quick and breezy
And always easy
Playing romantic games.

I wined and dined a thousand exotic Joans and Janes
In dusty dance halls, at debutante balls,
On lonely country lanes.
I fell in love forever,
Twice every year or so.
I wooed them sweetly, was theirs completely,
But they always let me go.
Saying bye now, no need to try now,
You don't have the proper charms.
Too sentimental and much too gentle
I don't tremble in your arms.

Then you rose into my life
Like a promised sunrise.
Brightening my days with the light in your eyes.
I've never been so strong,
Now I'm where I belong.

Phenomenal Woman

Pretty women wonder where my secret lies.
I'm not cute or built to suit a fashion model's size
But when I start to tell them,
They think I'm telling lies.
I say,
It's in the reach of my arms,
The span of my hips,
The stride of my step,
The curl of my lips.
I'm a woman
Phenomenally.
Phenomenal woman,
That's me.

I walk into a room
Just as cool as you please,
And to a man,
The fellows stand or
Fall down on their knees.
Then they swarm around me,
A hive of honey bees.
I say,
It's the fire in my eyes,
And the flash of my teeth,
The swing in my waist,
And the joy in my feet.
I'm a woman
Phenomenally.
Phenomenal woman,
That's me.

Men themselves have wondered
What they see in me.
They try so much
But they can't touch
My inner mystery.
When I try to show them,
They say they still can't see.
I say,
It's in the arch of my back,
The sun of my smile,
The ride of my breasts,
The grace of my style.
I'm a woman
Phenomenally.
Phenomenal woman,
That's me.

Now you understand
Just why my head's not bowed.
I don't shout or jump about
Or have to talk real loud.
When you see me passing,
It ought to make you proud.
I say,
It's in the click of my heels,
The bend of my hair,
the palm of my hand,
The need for my care.
'Cause I'm a woman
Phenomenally.
Phenomenal woman,
That's me.

Men

When I was young, I used to
Watch behind the curtains
As men walked up and down
The street. Wino men, old men.
Young men sharp as mustard.
See them. Men are always
Going somewhere.
They knew I was there. Fifteen
Years old and starving for them.
Under my window, they would pause,
Their shoulders high like the
Breasts of a young girl,
Jacket tails slapping over
Those behinds,
Men.
One day they hold you in the
Palms of their hands, gentle, as if you
Were the last raw egg in the world. Then
They tighten up. Just a little. The
First squeeze is nice. A quick hug.
Soft into your defenselessness. A little
More. The hurt begins. Wrench out a
Smile that slides around the fear. When the
Air disappears,
Your mind pops, exploding fiercely, briefly,
Like the head of a kitchen match. Shattered.
It is your juice
That runs down their legs. Staining their shoes.

When the earth rights itself again,
And taste tries to return to
    the tongue,
Your body has slammed shut. Forever.
No keys exist.

Then the window draws full upon
Your mind. There, just beyond
The sway of curtains, men walk.
Knowing something.
Going someplace.
But this time, you will simply
Stand and watch.

Maybe.

Refusal

Beloved,
In what other lives or lands
Have I known your lips
Your hands
Your laughter brave
Irreverent.
Those sweet excesses that
I do adore.
What surety is there
That we will meet again,
On other worlds some
Future time undated.
I defy my body's haste.
Without the Promise
Of one more sweet encounter
I will not deign to die.

Just for a Time

Oh how you used to walk
With that insouciant smile
I liked to hear you talk
And your style
Pleased me for a while.

You were my early love
New as a day breaking in Spring
You were the image of
Everything
That caused me to sing.

I don't like reminiscing
Nostalgia is not my forte
I don't spill tears
On yesterday's years
But honesty makes me say,
You were a precious pearl
How I loved to see you shine,
You were the perfect girl.
And you were mine.
For a time.
For a time.
Just for a time.

PART TWO

—

TRAVELING

Junkie Monkey Reel

Shoulders sag,
The pull of weighted needling.
Arms drag, smacking wet in soft bone
Sockets.

Knees thaw,
Their familiar magic lost. Old bend and
Lock and bend forgot.

Teeth rock in fetid gums.
Eyes dart, die, then float in
Simian juice.

Brains reel,
Master charts of old ideas erased. The
Routes are gone beneath the tracks
Of desert caravans, pre-slavery
Years ago.

Dreams fail,
Unguarded fears on homeward streets
Embrace. Throttling in a dark revenge
Murder is its sweet romance.

How long will
This monkey dance?

The Lesson

I keep on dying again.
Veins collapse, opening like the
Small fists of sleeping
Children.
Memory of old tombs,
Rotting flesh and worms do
Not convince me against
The challenge. The years
And cold defeat live deep in
Lines along my face.
They dull my eyes, yet
I keep on dying,
Because I love to live.

California Prodigal

FOR DAVID P-B

The eye follows, the land
Slips upward, creases down, forms
The gentle buttocks of a young
Giant. In the nestle,
Old adobe bricks, washed of
Whiteness, paled to umber,
Await another century.

Star Jasmine and old vines
Lay claim upon the ghosted land,
Then quiet pools whisper
Private childhood secrets.

Flush on inner cottage walls
Antiquitous faces,
Used to the gelid breath
Of old manors, glare disdainfully
Over breached time.

Around and through these
Cold phantasmatalities,
He walks, insisting
To the languid air,
Activity, music,
A generosity of graces.

His lupin fields spurn old
Deceit and agile poppies dance
In golden riot. Each day is

Fulminant, exploding brightly
Under the gaze of his exquisite
Sires, frozen in the famed paint
Of dead masters. Audacious
Sunlight casts defiance
At their feet.

My Arkansas

There is a deep brooding
in Arkansas.
Old crimes like moss pend
from poplar trees.
The sullen earth
is much too
red for comfort.

Sunrise seems to hesitate
and in that second
lose its
incandescent aim, and
dusk no more shadows
than the noon.
The past is brighter yet.

Old hates and
ante-bellum lace are rent
but not discarded.
Today is yet to come
in Arkansas.
It writhes. It writhes in awful
waves of brooding.

Through the Inner City to the Suburbs

Secured by sooted windows
And amazement, it is
Delicious. Frosting filched
From a company cake.

People. Black and fast. Scattered
Watermelon seeds on
A summer street. Grinning in
Ritual, sassy in pomp.

From a slow-moving train
They are precious. Stolen gems
Unsaleable and dear. Those
Dusky undulations sweat of forest
Nights, damp dancing, the juicy
Secrets of black thighs.

Images framed picture perfect
Do not move beyond the window
Siding.

Strong delectation:
Dirty stories in changing rooms
Accompany the slap of wet towels and
Toilet seats.
Poli-talk of politician
Parents: "They need shoes and
Cooze and a private
Warm latrine. I had a colored
Mammy . . ."

The train, bound for green lawns
Double garages and sullen women
In dreaded homes, settles down
On its habit track.
Leaving
The dark figures dancing
And grinning. Still
Grinning.

Lady Luncheon Club

Her counsel was accepted: the times are grave.
A man was needed who would make them think,
And pay him from the petty cash account.

Our woman checked her golden watch,
The speaker has a plane to catch.
Dessert is served (and just in time).

The lecturer leans, thrusts forth his head
And neck and chest, arms akimbo
On the lectern top. He summons up
Sincerity as one might call a favored
Pet.

He understands the female rage,
Why Eve was lustful and
Delilah's
Grim deceit.

Our woman thinks:
(This cake is much too sweet).

He sighs for youthful death
And rape at ten, and murder of
The soul stretched over long.

Our woman notes:
(This coffee's much too strong).

The jobless streets of
Wine and wandering when
Mornings promise no bright relief.

She claps her hands and writes
Upon her pad: (Next time the
Speaker must be brief).

Momma Welfare Roll

Her arms semaphore fat triangles,
Pudgy hands bunched on layered hips
Where bones idle under years of fatback
And lima beans.
Her jowls shiver in accusation
Of crimes clichéd by
Repetition. Her children, strangers
To childhood's toys, play
Best the games of darkened doorways,
Rooftop tag, and know the slick feel of
Other people's property.

Too fat to whore,
Too mad to work,
Searches her dreams for the
Lucky sign and walks bare-handed
Into a den of bureaucrats for
Her portion.
"They don't give me welfare.
I take it."

The Singer Will Not Sing

FOR A.L.

A benison given. Unused,
no angels promised,
wings fluttering banal lies
behind their sexlessness. No
trumpets gloried
prophecies of fabled fame.
Yet harmonies waited in
her stiff throat. New notes
lay expectant on her
stilled tongue.

Her lips are ridged and
fleshy. Purpled night birds
snuggled to rest.
The mouth seamed, voiceless.
Sounds do not lift beyond
those reddened walls.

She came too late and lonely
to this place.

Willie

Willie was a man without fame,
Hardly anybody knew his name.
Crippled and limping, always walking lame,
He said, "I keep on movin'
Movin' just the same."

Solitude was the climate in his head,
Emptiness was the partner in his bed,
Pain echoed in the steps of his tread,
He said, "I keep on followin'
Where the leaders led.

"I may cry and I will die,
But my spirit is the soul of every spring,
Watch for me and you will see
That I'm present in the songs that children sing."

People called him "Uncle," "Boy" and "Hey,"
Said, "You can't live through this another day."
Then, they waited to hear what he would say.
He said, "I'm living
In the games that children play.

"You may enter my sleep, people my dreams,
Threaten my early morning's ease,
But I keep comin' followin' laughin' cryin',
Sure as a summer breeze.

"Wait for me, watch for me.
My spirit is the surge of open seas.
Look for me, ask for me,
I'm the rustle in the autumn leaves.

"When the sun rises
I am the time.
When the children sing
I am the Rhyme."

To Beat the Child Was Bad Enough

A young body, light
As winter sunshine, a new
Seed's bursting promise,
Hung from a string of silence
Above its future.
(The chance of choice was never known.)
Hunger, new hands, strange voices,
Its cry came natural, tearing.

Water boiled in innocence, gaily
In a cheap pot.
The child exchanged its
Curiosity for terror. The skin
Withdrew, the flesh submitted.

Now, cries make shards
Of broken air, beyond an unremembered
Hunger and the peace of strange hands.

A young body floats.
Silently.

Woman Work

I've got the children to tend
The clothes to mend
The floor to mop
The food to shop
Then the chicken to fry
The baby to dry
I got company to feed
The garden to weed
I've got the shirts to press
The tots to dress
The cane to be cut
I gotta clean up this hut
Then see about the sick
And the cotton to pick.

Shine on me, sunshine
Rain on me, rain
Fall softly, dewdrops
And cool my brow again.

Storm, blow me from here
With your fiercest wind
Let me float across the sky
Till I can rest again.

Fall gently, snowflakes
Cover me with white
Cold icy kisses and
Let me rest tonight.

Sun, rain, curving sky
Mountain, oceans, leaf and stone
Star shine, moon glow
You're all that I can call my own.

One More Round

There ain't no pay beneath the sun
As sweet as rest when a job's well done.
I was born to work up to my grave
But I was not born
To be a slave.

One more round
And let's heave it down,
One more round
And let's heave it down.

Papa drove steel and Momma stood guard,
I never heard them holler 'cause the work was hard.
They were born to work up to their graves
But they were not born
To be worked-out slaves.

One more round
And let's heave it down,
One more round
And let's heave it down.

Brothers and sisters know the daily grind,
It was not labor made them lose their minds.
They were born to work up to their graves
But they were not born
To be worked-out slaves.

One more round
And let's heave it down,
One more round
And let's heave it down.

And now I'll tell you my Golden Rule,
I was born to work but I ain't no mule.
I was born to work up to my grave
But I was not born
To be a slave.

One more round
And let's heave it down,
One more round
And let's heave it down.

The Traveler

Byways and bygone
And lone nights long
Sun rays and sea waves
And star and stone

Manless and friendless
No cave my home
This is my torture
My long nights, lone

Kin

FOR BAILEY

We were entwined in red rings
Of blood and loneliness before
The first snows fell
Before muddy rivers seeded clouds
Above a virgin forest, and
Men ran naked, blue and black
Skinned into the warm embraces
Of Sheba, Eve and Lilith.
I was your sister.

You left me to force strangers
Into brother molds, exacting
Taxations they never
Owed or could ever pay.

You fought to die, thinking
In destruction lies the seed
Of birth. You may be right.

I will remember silent walks in
Southern woods and long talks
In low voices
Shielding meaning from the big ears
Of overcurious adults.

You may be right.
Your slow return from
Regions of terror and bloody
Screams, races my heart.

I hear again the laughter
Of children and see fireflies
Bursting tiny explosions in
An Arkansas twilight.

The Memory

Cotton rows crisscross the world
    And dead-tired nights of yearning
Thunderbolts on leather strops
    And all my body burning

Sugar cane reach up to God
    And every baby crying
Shame the blanket of my night
    And all my days are dying

PART THREE

—

AND STILL
I RISE

Still I Rise

You may write me down in history
With your bitter, twisted lies,
You may trod me in the very dirt
But still, like dust, I'll rise.

Does my sassiness upset you?
Why are you beset with gloom?
'Cause I walk like I've got oil wells
Pumping in my living room.

Just like moons and like suns,
With the certainty of tides,
Just like hopes springing high,
Still I'll rise.

Did you want to see me broken?
Bowed head and lowered eyes?
Shoulders falling down like teardrops,
Weakened by my soulful cries?

Does my haughtiness offend you?
Don't you take it awful hard
'Cause I laugh like I've got gold mines
Diggin' in my own backyard.

You may shoot me with your words,
You may cut me with your eyes,
You may kill me with your hatefulness,
But still, like air, I'll rise.

Does my sexiness upset you?
Does it come as a surprise

That I dance like I've got diamonds
At the meeting of my thighs?

Out of the huts of history's shame
I rise
Up from a past that's rooted in pain
I rise
I'm a black ocean, leaping and wide,
Welling and swelling I bear in the tide.

Leaving behind nights of terror and fear
I rise
Into a daybreak that's wondrously clear
I rise
Bringing the gifts that my ancestors gave,
I am the dream and the hope of the slave.
I rise
I rise
I rise.

Ain't That Bad?

Dancin' the funky chicken
Eatin' ribs and tips
Diggin' all the latest sounds
And drinkin' gin in sips.

Puttin' down that do-rag
Tightenin' up my 'fro
Wrappin' up in Blackness
Don't I shine and glow?

Hearin' Stevie Wonder
Cookin' beans and rice
Goin' to the opera
Checkin' out Leontyne Price.

Get down, Jesse Jackson
Dance on, Alvin Ailey
Talk, Miss Barbara Jordan
Groove, Miss Pearlie Bailey.

Now ain't they bad?
An' ain't they Black?
An' ain't they Black?
An' ain't they bad?
An' ain't they bad?
An' ain't they Black?
An' ain't they fine?

Black like the hour of the night
When your love turns and wriggles close to your side
Black as the earth which has given birth
To nations, and when all else is gone will abide.

Bad as the storm that leaps raging from the heavens
Bringing the welcome rain
Bad as the sun burning orange hot at midday
Lifting the waters again.

Arthur Ashe on the tennis court
Mohammed Ali in the ring
André Watts and Andrew Young
Black men doing their thing.

Dressing in purples and pinks and greens
Exotic as rum and Cokes
Living our lives with flash and style
Ain't we colorful folks?

Now ain't we bad?
An' ain't we Black?
An' ain't we Black?
An' ain't we bad?
An' ain't we bad?
An' ain't we Black?
An' ain't we fine?

Life Doesn't Frighten Me

Shadows on the wall
Noises down the hall
Life doesn't frighten me at all
Bad dogs barking loud
Big ghosts in a cloud
Life doesn't frighten me at all.

Mean old Mother Goose
Lions on the loose
They don't frighten me at all
Dragons breathing flame
On my counterpane
That doesn't frighten me at all.

I go boo
Make them shoo
I make fun
Way they run
I won't cry
So they fly
I just smile
They go wild
Life doesn't frighten me at all.

Tough guys in a fight
All alone at night
Life doesn't frighten me at all.
Panthers in the park
Strangers in the dark
No, they don't frighten me at all.

That new classroom where
Boys all pull my hair
(Kissy little girls
With their hair in curls)
They don't frighten me at all.

Don't show me frogs and snakes
And listen for my scream,
If I'm afraid at all
It's only in my dreams.

I've got a magic charm
That I keep up my sleeve,
I can walk the ocean floor
And never have to breathe.

Life doesn't frighten me at all
Not at all
Not at all.
Life doesn't frighten me at all.

Bump d'Bump

Play me a game like Blind Man's dance
And bind my eyes with ignorance
Bump d'bump bump d'bump.

Tell my life with a liquor sign
Or a cooking spoon from the five-and-dime
And a junkie reel in two/four time
Bump d'bump bump d'bump.

Call me a name from an ugly south
Like liver lips and satchel mouth
Bump d'bump bump d'bump.

I'll play possum and close my eyes
To your greater sins and my lesser lies
That way I share my nation's prize
Bump d'bump bump d'bump.

I may be last in the welfare line
Below the rim where the sun don't shine
But getting up stays on my mind
Bump d'bump bump d'bump.

On Aging

When you see me sitting quietly,
Like a sack left on the shelf,
Don't think I need your chattering.
I'm listening to myself.
Hold! Stop! Don't pity me!
Hold! Stop your sympathy!
Understanding if you got it,
Otherwise I'll do without it!

When my bones are stiff and aching,
And my feet won't climb the stair,
I will only ask one favor:
Don't bring me no rocking chair.

When you see me walking, stumbling,
Don't study and get it wrong.
'Cause tired don't mean lazy
And every goodbye ain't gone.
I'm the same person I was back then,
A little less hair, a little less chin,
A lot less lungs and much less wind.
But ain't I lucky I can still breathe in.

In Retrospect

Last year changed its seasons
subtly, stripped its sultry winds
for the reds of dying leaves, let
gelid drips of winter ice melt onto a
warming earth and urged the dormant
bulbs to brave the
pain of spring.

•

We, loving, above the whim of
time, did not notice.

Alone. I remember now.

Just Like Job

My Lord, my Lord,
Long have I cried out to Thee
In the heat of the sun,
The cool of the moon,
My screams searched the heavens for Thee.
My God,
When my blanket was nothing but dew,
Rags and bones
Were all I owned,
I chanted Your name
Just like Job.

Father, Father,
My life give I gladly to Thee
Deep rivers ahead
High mountains above
My soul wants only Your love
But fears gather round like wolves in the dark.
Have You forgotten my name?
O Lord, come to Your child.
O Lord, forget me not.

You said to lean on Your arm
And I'm leaning
You said to trust in Your love
And I'm trusting
You said to call on Your name
And I'm calling
I'm stepping out on Your word.

You said You'd be my protection,
My only and glorious saviour,

My beautiful Rose of Sharon,
And I'm stepping out on Your word.
Joy, joy
Your word.
Joy, joy
The wonderful word of the Son of God.

You said that You would take me to glory
To sit down at the welcome table
Rejoice with my mother in heaven
And I'm stepping out on Your word.

Into the alleys
Into the byways
Into the streets
And the roads
And the highways
Past rumor mongers
And midnight ramblers
Past the liars and the cheaters and the gamblers
On Your word
On Your word.
On the wonderful word of the Son of God.
I'm stepping out on Your word.

Call Letters: Mrs. V. B.

Ships?
Sure I'll sail them.
Show me the boat,
If it'll float,
I'll sail it.

Men?
Yes I'll love them.
If they've got the style,
To make me smile,
I'll love them.

Life?
'Course I'll live it.
Let me have breath,
Just to my death,
And I'll live it.

Failure?
I'm not ashamed to tell it,
I never learned to spell it.
Not Failure.

Thank You, Lord

I see You
Brown-skinned,
Neat Afro,
Full lips,
A little goatee.
A Malcolm,
Martin,
Du Bois.
Sunday services become sweeter when You're Black,
Then I don't have to explain why
I was out balling the town down,
Saturday night.

Thank you, Lord.
I want to thank You, Lord,
For life and all that's in it.
Thank You for the day
And for the hour and for the minute.
I know many are gone,
I'm still living on,
I want to thank You.

I went to sleep last night
And I arose with the dawn,
I know that there are others
Who're still sleeping on,
They've gone away,
You've let me stay.
I want to thank You.

Some thought because they'd seen sunrise
They'd see it rise again.

But death crept into their sleeping beds
And took them by the hand.
Because of Your mercy,
I have another day to live.

Let me humbly say,
Thank You for this day
I want to thank You.

I was once a sinner man,
Living unsaved and wild,
Taking my chances in a dangerous world,
Putting my soul on trial.
Because of Your mercy,
Falling down on me like rain,
Because of Your mercy,
When I die I'll live again,
Let me humbly say,
Thank You for this day.
I want to thank You.

SHAKER, WHY DON'T YOU SING?

Another book

for

GUY JOHNSON

and

COLIN ASHANTI MURPHY JOHNSON

Thanks to

ELEANOR TRAYLOR

for her radiance

ELIZABETH PHILLIPS

for her art

RUTH BECKFORD

for her constancy

Awaking in New York

Curtains forcing their will
against the wind,
children sleep,
exchanging dreams with
seraphim. The city
drags itself awake on
subway straps; and
I, an alarm, awake as
a rumor of war,
lie stretching into dawn,
unasked and unheeded.

A Good Woman Feeling Bad

The blues may be the life you've led
Or midnight hours in
An empty bed. But persecuting
Blues I've known
Could stalk
Like tigers, break like bone,

Pend like rope in
A gallows tree,
Make me curse
My pedigree,

Bitterness thick on
A rankling tongue,
A psalm to love that's
Left unsung,

Rivers heading north
But ending South,
Funeral music
In a going-home mouth.

All riddles are blues,
And all blues are sad,
And I'm only mentioning
Some blues I've had.

The Health-Food Diner

No sprouted wheat and soya shoots
And brussels in a cake,
Carrot straw and spinach raw
(Today, I need a steak).

Not thick brown rice and rice pilau
Or mushrooms creamed on toast,
Turnips mashed and parsnips hashed
(I'm dreaming of a roast).

Health-food folks around the world
Are thinned by anxious zeal,
They look for help in seafood kelp
(I count on breaded veal).

No Smoking signs, raw mustard greens,
Zucchini by the ton,
Uncooked kale and bodies frail
Are sure to make me run

to

Loins of pork and chicken thighs
And standing rib, so prime,
Pork chops brown and fresh ground round
(I crave them all the time).

Irish stews and boiled corned beef
And hot dogs by the scores,
Or any place that saves a space
For smoking carnivores.

A Georgia Song

We swallow the odors of Southern cities,
Fatback boiled to submission,
Tender evening poignancies of
Magnolia and the great green
Smell of fresh sweat.
In Southern fields,
The sound of distant
Feet running, or dancing,
And the liquid notes of
Sorrow songs,
Waltzes, screams and
French quadrilles float over
The loam of Georgia.

Sing me to sleep, Savannah.

Clocks run down in Tara's halls and dusty
Flags droop their unbearable
Sadness.

Remember our days, Susannah.

Oh, the blood-red clay,
Wet still with ancient
Wrongs, and Abenaa
Singing her Creole airs to
Macon.
We long, dazed, for winter evenings
And a whitened moon,
And the snap of controllable fires.

Cry for our souls, Augusta.

We need a wind to strike
Sharply, as the thought of love
Betrayed can stop the heart.
An absence of tactile
Romance, no lips offering
Succulence, nor eyes
Rolling, disconnected from
A Sambo face.

Dare us new dreams, Columbus.

A cool new moon, a
Winter's night, calm blood,
Sluggish, moving only
Out of habit, we need
Peace.

O Atlanta, O deep, and
Once-lost city,

Chant for us a new song. A song
Of Southern peace.

Unmeasured Tempo

The sun rises at midday.
Nubile breasts sag to waistlines while
young loins grow dull,
so late.
Dreams are petted, like
cherished lapdogs
misunderstood and loved
too well.

Much knowledge
wrinkles the cerebellum,
but little informs.
Leaps are
made into narrow mincings.
Great desires strain
into petty wishes.
You did arrive, smiling,
but too late.

Amoebaean for Daddy

I was a pretty baby.
White folks used to stop
My mother
Just to look at me.
(All black babies
Are Cute.) Mother called me
Bootsie and Daddy said . . .
(Nobody listened to him).

On the Union Pacific, a
Dining-car waiter, bowing and scraping,
Momma told him to
Stand up straight, he shamed her
In the big house
(Bought from tips) in front of her
Nice club ladies.

His short legs were always
Half bent. He could have posed as
The Black jockey Mother found
And put on the lawn.
He sat silent when
We ate from the good railroad china
And stolen silver spoons.
Furniture crowded our
Lonely house.

But I was young and played
In the evenings under a blanket of
Licorice sky. When Daddy came home
(I might be forgiven) that last night,
I had been running in the

Big backyard and
Stood sweating above the tired old man,
Panting like a young horse,
Impatient with his lingering. He said
"All I ever asked, all I ever asked, all I ever—"
Daddy, you should have died
Long before I was a
Pretty baby, and white
Folks used to stop
Just to look at me.

Recovery

FOR DUGALD

A last love,
proper in conclusion,
should snip the wings,
forbidding further flight.

But I, now,
reft of that confusion,
am lifted up
and speeding toward the light.

Impeccable Conception

I met a Lady Poet
who took for inspiration
colored birds, and whispered words,
a lover's hesitation.

A falling leaf could stir her.
A wilting, dying rose
would make her write, both day and night,
the most rewarding prose.

She'd find a hidden meaning
in every pair of pants,
then hurry home to be alone
and write about romance.

Caged Bird

A free bird leaps
on the back of the wind
and floats downstream
till the current ends
and dips his wing
in the orange sun rays
and dares to claim the sky.

But a bird that stalks
down his narrow cage
can seldom see through
his bars of rage
his wings are clipped and
his feet are tied
so he opens his throat to sing.

The caged bird sings
with a fearful trill
of things unknown
but longed for still
and his tune is heard
on the distant hill
for the caged bird
sings of freedom.

The free bird thinks of another breeze
and the trade winds soft through the sighing trees
and the fat worms waiting on a dawn-bright lawn
and he names the sky his own.

But a caged bird stands on the grave of dreams
his shadow shouts on a nightmare scream

his wings are clipped and his feet are tied
so he opens his throat to sing.

The caged bird sings
with a fearful trill
of things unknown
but longed for still
and his tune is heard
on the distant hill
for the caged bird
sings of freedom.

Avec Merci, Mother

From her perch of beauty
posing lofty,
Sustained upon the plaudits
of the crowd,

She praises all who kneel and
whispers softly,
"A genuflection's better
with head bowed."

Among the mass of people
who adore her
A solitary figure
holds her eyes.

His salty tears invoke
her sweet reaction,
"He's so much like his daddy
when he cries."

Arrival

Angels gather.
The rush of mad air
cyclones through.
Wing tips brush the
hair, a million
strands
stand; waving black anemones.
Hosannahs crush the
shell's ear tender, and
tremble
down clattering
to the floor.
Harps sound,
undulate their
sensuous meanings.
Hallelujah! Hallelujah!
You
beyond the door.

A Plagued Journey

There is no warning rattle at the door
nor heavy feet to stomp the foyer boards.
Safe in the dark prison, I know that
light slides over
the fingered work of a toothless
woman in Pakistan.
Happy prints of
an invisible time are illumined.
My mouth agape
rejects the solid air and
lungs hold. The invader takes
direction and
seeps through the plaster walls.
It is at my chamber, entering
the keyhole, pushing
through the padding of the door.
I cannot scream. A bone
of fear clogs my throat.
It is upon me. It is
sunrise, with Hope
its arrogant rider.
My mind, formerly quiescent
in its snug encasement, is strained
to look upon their rapturous visages,
to let them enter even into me.
I am forced
outside myself to
mount the light and ride joined with Hope.
Through all the bright hours
I cling to expectation, until
darkness comes to reclaim me
as its own. Hope fades, day is gone

into its irredeemable place
and I am thrown back into the familiar
bonds of disconsolation.
Gloom crawls around
lapping lasciviously
between my toes, at my ankles,
and it sucks the strands of my
hair. It forgives my heady
fling with Hope. I am
joined again into its
greedy arms.

Starvation

Hurray! Hurry!
Come through the keyhole.
Don't mind the rotting
sashes, pass into the windows.
Come, good news.

I'm holding my apron
to catch your plumpness.
The largest pot shines
with happiness. The slack
walls of my purse, pulsing
pudenda, await you with
a new bride's longing.
The bread bin gapes and
the oven holds its cold
breath.
Hurry up! Hurry down!
Good tidings. Don't wait
out my misery. Do not play
coy with my longing.

Hunger has grown old and
ugly with me. We hate from
too much knowing. Come.
Press out this sour beast which
fills the bellies of my children
and laughs at each eviction notice.
Come!

Contemporary Announcement

Ring the big bells,
cook the cow,
put on your silver locket.
The landlord is knocking at the door
and I've got the rent in my pocket.

Douse the lights,
hold your breath,
take my heart in your hand.
I lost my job two weeks ago
and rent day's here again.

Prelude to a Parting

Beside you, prone,
my naked skin finds
fault in touching.
Yet it is you
who draws away.
The tacit fact is:
the awful fear of losing
is not enough to cause
a fleeing love
to stay.

Martial Choreograph

Hello, young sailor.
You are betrayed and
do not know the dance of death.
Dandy warrior, swaying to
Rick James on your
stereo, you do not hear the
bleat of triumphant war, its
roar is not in
your ears, filled with Stevie Wonder.

"Show me how to do like you.
Show me how to do it."

You will be surprised that
trees grunt when torn from
their root sockets to fandango into dust,
and exploding bombs force a lively Lindy
on grasses and frail bodies.

Go galloping on, bopping,
in the airport, young sailor.
Your body, virgin
still, has not swung the bloody buck-and-wing.
Manhood is a newly delivered
message. Your eyes,
rampant as an open city,
have not yet seen life steal from
limbs outstretched and trembling
like the arms of dancers
and dying swans.

To a Suitor

If you are Black and for me,
press steady, as the weight
of night. And I will show
cascades of brilliance, astrally.

If you are Black and constant,
descend importantly,
as ritual, and I will arch
a crescent moon, naturally.

Insomniac

There are some nights when
sleep plays coy,
aloof and disdainful.
And all the wiles
that I employ to win
its service to my side
are useless as wounded pride,
and much more painful.

Weekend Glory

Some dichty folks
don't know the facts,
posin' and preenin'
and puttin' on acts,
stretchin' their necks
and strainin' their backs.

They move into condos
up over the ranks,
pawn their souls
to the local banks.
Buyin' big cars
they can't afford,
ridin' around town
actin' bored.

If they want to learn how to live life right,
they ought to study me on Saturday night.

My job at the plant
ain't the biggest bet,
but I pay my bills
and stay out of debt.
I get my hair done
for my own self's sake,
so I don't have to pick
and I don't have to rake.

Take the church money out
and head cross town
to my friend girl's house
where we plan our round.

We meet our men and go to a joint
where the music is blues
and to the point.

Folks write about me.
They just can't see
how I work all week
at the factory.
Then get spruced up
and laugh and dance
and turn away from worry
with sassy glance.

They accuse me of livin'
from day to day,
but who are they kiddin'?
So are they.

My life ain't heaven
but it sure ain't hell.
I'm not on top
but I call it swell
if I'm able to work
and get paid right
and have the luck to be Black
on a Saturday night.

The Lie

Today, you threaten to leave me.
I hold curses, in my mouth,
which could flood your path, sear
bottomless chasms in your road.

I keep, behind my lips,
invectives capable of tearing
the septum from your
nostrils and the skin from your back.

Tears, copious as a spring rain,
are checked in ducts
and screams are crowded in a corner
of my throat.

You are leaving?

Aloud, I say:
I'll help you pack, but it's getting late,
I have to hurry or miss my date.
When I return, I know you'll be gone.
Do drop a line or telephone.

Prescience

Had I known that the heart
breaks slowly, dismantling itself
into unrecognizable plots of
misery,

Had I known the heart would leak,
slobbering its sap, with a vulgar
visibility, into the dressed-up
dining rooms of strangers,

Had I known that solitude could
stifle the breath, loosen the joint,
and force the tongue against the
palate,

Had I known that loneliness could
keloid, winding itself around the
body in an ominous and beautiful
cicatrix,

Had I known, yet I would have loved
you, your brash and insolent beauty,
your heavy comedic face
and knowledge of sweet
delights,

But from a distance.
I would have left you whole and wholly
for the delectation of those who
wanted more and cared less.

Family Affairs

You let down, from arched
Windows,
Over hand-cut stones of your
Cathedrals, seas of golden hair.

While I, pulled by dusty braids,
Left furrows in the
Sands of African beaches.

Princes and commoners
Climbed over waves to reach
Your vaulted boudoirs,

As the sun, capriciously,
Struck silver fire from waiting
Chains, where I was bound.

My screams never reached
The rare tower where you
Lay, birthing masters for
My sons, and for my
Daughters, a swarm of
Unclean badgers, to consume
Their history.

Tired now of pedestal existence
For fear of flying
And vertigo, you descend
And step lightly over
My centuries of horror
And take my hand,

Smiling, call me
          Sister.

Sister, accept
That I must wait a
While. Allow an age
Of dust to fill
Ruts left on my
Beach in Africa.

Changes

Fickle comfort steals away
What it knows
It will not say
What it can
It will not do
It flies from me
To humor you.

Capricious peace will not bind
The severed nerves
The jagged mind
The shattered dream
The loveless sleep
It frolics now
Within your keep.

Confidence, that popinjay,
Is planning now
To slip away
Look fast
It's fading rapidly
Tomorrow it returns to me.

Brief Innocence

Dawn offers
innocence to a half-mad city.

The axe-keen
intent of all our
days for this brief
moment lies soft, nuzzling
the breast of morning,
crooning, still sleep-besotted,
of childish pranks with
angels.

The Last Decision

The print is too small, distressing me.
Wavering black things on the page.
Wriggling polliwogs all about.
I know it's my age.
I'll have to give up reading.

The food is too rich, revolting me.
I swallow it hot or force it down cold,
and wait all day as it sits in my throat.
Tired as I am, I know I've grown old.
I'll have to give up eating.

My children's concerns are tiring me.
They stand at my bed and move their lips,
and I cannot hear one single word.
I'd rather give up listening.

Life is too busy, wearying me.
Questions and answers and heavy thought.
I've subtracted and added and multiplied,
and all my figuring has come to naught.
Today I'll give up living.

Slave Coffle

Just Beyond my reaching,
　an itch away from fingers,
　was the river bed
　and the high road home.

Now Beneath my walking,
　solid down to China,
　all the earth is horror
　and the dark night long.

Then Before the dawning,
　bright as grinning demons,
　came the fearful knowledge
　that my life was gone.

Shaker, Why Don't You Sing?

Evicted from sleep's mute palace,
I wait in silence
for the bridal croon;
your legs rubbing insistent
rhythm against my thighs,
your breath moaning
a canticle in my hair.
But the solemn moments,
unuttering, pass in
unaccompanied procession.
You, whose chanteys hummed
my life alive, have withdrawn
your music and lean inaudibly
on the quiet slope of memory.

O Shaker, why don't you sing?

In the night noisy with
street cries and the triumph
of amorous insects, I focus beyond
those cacophonies for
the anthem of your hands and swelling chest,
for the perfect harmonies which are
your lips. Yet darkness brings
no syncopated promise. I rest somewhere
between the unsung notes of night.

Shaker, why don't you sing?

My Life Has Turned to Blue

Our summer's gone,
the golden days are through.
The rosy dawns I used to
wake with you
have turned to grey,
my life has turned to blue.

The once-green lawns
glisten now with dew.
Red robin's gone,
down to the South he flew.
Left here alone,
my life has turned to blue.

I've heard the news
that winter too will pass,
that spring's a sign
that summer's due at last.
But until I see you
lying in green grass,
my life has turned to blue.

I SHALL NOT

BE MOVED

VIVIAN BAXTER

MILDRED GARRIS TUTTLE

Worker's Song

Big ships shudder
down to the sea
    because of me
Railroads run
on a twinness track
    'cause of my back
    Whoppa, Whoppa
    Whoppa, Whoppa

Cars stretch to
a super length
    'cause of my strength
Planes fly high
over seas and lands
    'cause of my hands
    Whoppa, Whoppa
    Whoppa, Whoppa

I wake
start the factory humming
I work late
keep the whole world running
and I got something . . . something
coming . . . coming. . . .
    Whoppa
    Whoppa
    Whoppa

Human Family

I note the obvious differences
in the human family.
Some of us are serious,
some thrive on comedy.

Some declare their lives are lived
as true profundity,
and others claim they really live
the real reality.

The variety of our skin tones
can confuse, bemuse, delight,
brown and pink and beige and purple,
tan and blue and white.

I've sailed upon the seven seas
and stopped in every land,
I've seen the wonders of the world,
not yet one common man.

I know ten thousand women
called Jane and Mary Jane,
but I've not seen any two
who really were the same.

Mirror twins are different
although their features jibe,
and lovers think quite different thoughts
while lying side by side.

We love and lose in China,
we weep on England's moors,

and laugh and moan in Guinea,
and thrive on Spanish shores.

We seek success in Finland,
are born and die in Maine.
In minor ways we differ,
in major we're the same.

I note the obvious differences
between each sort and type,
but we are more alike, my friends,
than we are unalike.

We are more alike, my friends,
than we are unalike.

We are more alike, my friends,
than we are unalike.

Man Bigot

The man who is a bigot
is the worst thing God has got,
except his match, his woman,
who really is Ms. Begot.

Old Folks Laugh

They have spent their
content of simpering,
holding their lips this
and that way, winding
the lines between
their brows. Old folks
allow their bellies to jiggle like slow
tamborines.
The hollers
rise up and spill
over any way they want.
When old folks laugh, they free the world.
They turn slowly, slyly knowing
the best and worst
of remembering.
Saliva glistens in
the corners of their mouths,
their heads wobble
on brittle necks, but
their laps
are filled with memories.
When old folks laugh, they consider the promise
of dear painless death, and generously
forgive life for happening
to them.

Is Love

Midwives and winding sheets
know birthing is hard
and dying is mean
and living's a trial in between.

Why do we journey, muttering
like rumors among the stars?
Is a dimension lost?
Is it love?

Forgive

Take me, Virginia,
bind me close
with Jamestown memories
of camptown races and
ships pregnant
with certain cargo
and Richmond riding high on greed
and low on tedious tides
of guilt.

But take me on, Virginia,
loose your turban of flowers
that peach petals and
dogwood bloom may
form epaulettes of white
tenderness on my shoulders
and round my
head ringlets
of forgiveness, poignant
as rolled eyes, sad as summer
parasols in a hurricane.

Insignificant

A series of small, on
their own insignificant,
occurrences. Salt lost half
its savor. Two yellow-
striped bumblebees got
lost in my hair.
When I freed them they droned
away into the afternoon.

At the clinic the nurse's
face was half pity and part pride.
I was not glad for the news.
Then I thought I heard you
call, and I, running
like water, headed for
the railroad track. It was only
the Baltimore and the Atchison,
Topeka, and the Santa Fe.
Small insignificancies.

Love Letter

Listening winds
overhear my privacies
spoken aloud (in your
absence, but for your sake).

When you, mustachioed,
nutmeg-brown lotus,
sit beside the Oberlin shoji.

My thoughts are particular:
of your light lips and hungry
hands writing Tai Chi urgencies
into my body. I leap, float,
run

to spring cool springs into
your embrace. Then we match grace.
This girl, neither feather nor
fan, drifted and tossed.

Oh, but then I had power.
Power.

Equality

You declare you see me dimly
through a glass which will not shine,
though I stand before you boldly,
trim in rank and marking time.

You do own to hear me faintly
as a whisper out of range,
while my drums beat out the message
and the rhythms never change.

Equality, and I will be free.
Equality, and I will be free.

You announce my ways are wanton,
that I fly from man to man,
but if I'm just a shadow to you,
could you ever understand?

We have lived a painful history,
we know the shameful past,
but I keep on marching forward,
and you keep on coming last.

Equality, and I will be free.
Equality, and I will be free.

Take the blinders from your vision,
take the padding from your ears,
and confess you've heard me crying,
and admit you've seen my tears.

Hear the tempo so compelling,
hear the blood throb in my veins.
Yes, my drums are beating nightly,
and the rhythms never change.

Equality, and I will be free.
Equality, and I will be free.

Coleridge Jackson

Coleridge Jackson had nothing
to fear. He weighed sixty pounds
more than his sons and one
hundred pounds more than his wife.

His neighbors knew he wouldn't
take tea for the fever.
The gents at the poolroom
walked gently in his presence.

So everyone used
to wonder why,
when his puny boss, a little
white bag of bones and
squinty eyes, when he frowned
at Coleridge, sneered at
the way Coleridge shifted
a ton of canned goods from
the east wall of the warehouse
all the way to the west,
when that skimpy piece of
man-meat called Coleridge
a sorry nigger,
Coleridge kept his lips closed,
sealed, jammed tight.
Wouldn't raise his eyes,
held his head at a slant,
looking way off somewhere
else.

Everybody in the neighborhood wondered
why Coleridge would come home,
pull off his jacket, take off
his shoes, and beat the
water and the will out of his puny
little family.

Everybody, even Coleridge, wondered
(the next day, or even later that
same night).
Everybody. But the weasly little
sack-of-bones boss with his
envious little eyes,
he knew. He always
knew. And
when people told him about
Coleridge's family, about the
black eyes and the bruised
faces, the broken bones,
Lord, how that scrawny man
grinned.

And the next
day, for a few hours, he treated
Coleridge nice. Like Coleridge
had just done him the biggest
old favor. Then, right
after lunch, he'd start on
Coleridge again.

"Here, Sambo, come here.
Can't you move any faster
than that? Who on earth
needs a lazy nigger?"
And Coleridge would just
stand there. His eyes sliding
away, lurking at something else.

Why Are They Happy People?

Skin back your teeth, damn you,
wiggle your ears,
laugh while the years
race
down your face.

Pull up your cheeks, black boy,
wrinkle your nose,
grin as your toes
spade
up your grave.

Roll those big eyes, black gal,
rubber your knees,
smile when the trees
bend
with your kin.

Son to Mother

I start no
wars, raining poison
on cathedrals,
melting Stars of David
into golden faucets
to be lighted by lamps
shaded by human skin.

I set no
store on the strange lands,
send no
missionaries beyond my
borders,
to plunder secrets
and barter souls.

They
say you took my manhood,
Momma.
Come sit on my lap
and tell me,
what do you want me to say
to them, just
before I annihilate
their ignorance?

Known to Eve and Me

His tan and golden self,
coiled in a threadbare carapace,
beckoned to my sympathy.
I hoisted him, shoulders above
the crowded plaza, lifting
his cool, slick body toward the altar of
sunlight. He was guileless, and slid into my embrace.
We shared seeded rolls and breakfast on the mountaintop.
Love's warmth and Aton's sun
disc caressed
his skin, and once-dulled scales
became sugared ginger, amber
drops of beryl on the tongue.

His lidless eye slid sideways,
and he rose into my deepest
yearning, bringing
gifts of ready rhythms, and
hourly wound around
my chest,
holding me fast in taut
security.
Then, glistening like
diamonds strewn
upon a black girl's belly,
he left me. And nothing
remains. Beneath my left
breast, two perfect identical punctures,
through which I claim
the air I breathe and
the slithering sound of my own skin
moving in the dark.

These Yet to Be United States

Tremors of your network
cause kings to disappear.
Your open mouth in anger
makes nations bow in fear.
Your bombs can change the seasons,
obliterate the spring.
What more do you long for?
Why are you suffering?

You control the human lives
in Rome and Timbuktu.
Lonely nomads wandering
owe Telstar to you.
Seas shift at your bidding,
your mushrooms fill the sky.
Why are you unhappy?
Why do your children cry?

They kneel alone in terror
with dread in every glance.
Their nights are threatened daily
by a grim inheritance.
You dwell in whitened castles
with deep and poisoned moats
and cannot hear the curses
which fill your children's throats.

Me and My Work

I got a piece of a job on the waterfront.
Three days ain't hardly a grind.
It buys some beans and collard greens
and pays the rent on time.
   'Course the wife works too.

Got three big children to keep in school,
need clothes and shoes on their feet,
give them enough of the things they want
and keep them out of the street.
   They've always been good.

My story ain't news and it ain't all sad.
There's plenty worse off than me.
Yet the only thing I really don't need
is strangers' sympathy.
That's someone else's word for
   caring.

Changing

It occurs to me now,
I never see you smiling
anymore. Friends
praise your
humor rich, your phrases
turning on a thin
dime. For me your wit is honed
to killing sharpness.
But I never catch
you simply smiling, anymore.

Born That Way

As far as possible, she strove
for them all. Arching her small
frame and grunting
prettily, her
fingers counting the roses
in the wallpaper.

Childhood whoring fitted her
for deceit. Daddy had been a
fondler. Soft lipped mouthings,
soft lapped rubbings.
A smile for pretty shoes,
a kiss could earn a dress.
And a private telephone
was worth the biggest old caress.

The neighbors and family friends
whispered she was seen
walking up and down the streets
when she was seventeen.
No one asked her reasons.
She couldn't even say.
She just took for granted
she was born that way.

As far as possible, she strove
for them all. Arching her small
frame and grunting
prettily, her
fingers counting the roses
in the wallpaper.

Televised

Televised news turns
a half-used day into
a waste of desolation.
If nothing wondrous preceded
the catastrophic announcements,
certainly nothing will follow, save
the sad-eyed faces of
bony children,
distended bellies making
mock at their starvation.
Why are they always
Black?
Whom do they await?
The lamb-chop flesh
reeks and cannot be
eaten. Even the
green peas roll on my plate
unmolested. Their innocence
matched by the helpless
hope in the children's faces.
Why do Black children
hope? Who will bring
them peas and lamb chops
and one more morning?

Nothing Much

But of course you were
always nothing. No thing.
A red-hot rocket, patriotically
bursting in my
veins. Showers of stars—cascading stars
behind closed eyelids. A
searing brand across my
forehead. Nothing of importance.
A four-letter word stenciled
on the flesh of my inner
thigh.
Stomping through my brain's
mush valleys. Strewing a
halt of new loyalties.

My life, so I say
        nothing much.

Glory Falls

Glory falls around us
as we sob
a dirge of
desolation on the Cross
and hatred is the ballast of
the rock
        which lies upon our necks
        and underfoot.
We have woven
        robes of silk
        and clothed our nakedness
        with tapestry.
From crawling on this
        murky planet's floor
        we soar beyond the
        birds and
        through the clouds
        and edge our way from hate
        and blind despair and
        bring honor
        to our brothers, and to our sisters cheer.
We grow despite the
        horror that we feed
        upon our own
        tomorrow.
We grow.

London

If I remember correctly,
London is a very queer place.
Mighty queer.
A million miles from
jungle, and the British
lion roars in the stone of
Trafalgar Square.
Mighty queer.
At least a condition
removed from Calcutta,
but old men in Islington and in
too-large sweaters dream
of the sunrise days
of the British Raj.
Awfully queer.
Centuries of hate divide St. George's
channel and the Gaels,
but plum-cheeked English boys drink
sweet tea and grow to fight
for their Queen.
Mighty queer.

Savior

Petulant priests, greedy
centurions, and one million
incensed gestures stand
between your love and me.

Your *agape* sacrifice
is reduced to colored glass,
vapid penance, and the
tedium of ritual.

Your footprints yet
mark the crest of
billowing seas but
your joy
fades upon the tablets
of ordained prophets.

Visit us again, Savior.

Your children, burdened with
disbelief, blinded by a patina
of wisdom,
carom down this vale of
fear. We cry for you
although we have lost
your name.

Many and More

There are many and more
who would kiss my hand,
taste my lips,
to my loneliness lend
their bodies' warmth.

I have want of a friend.

There are few, some few,
who would give their names
and fortunes rich
or send first sons
to my ailing bed.

I have need of a friend.

There is one and only one
who will give the air
from his failing lungs
for my body's mend.

And that one is my love.

The New House

What words
have smashed against
these walls,
crashed up and down these
halls,
lain mute and then drained
their meanings out and into
these floors?

What feelings, long since
dead,
streamed vague yearnings
below this ceiling
light?
In some dimension,
which I cannot know,
the shadows of
another still exist. I bring my
memories, held too long in check,
to let them here shoulder
space and place to be.

And when I leave to
find another house,
I wonder, what among
these shades will be
left of me.

Our Grandmothers

She lay, skin down on the moist dirt,
the canebrake rustling
with the whispers of leaves, and
loud longing of hounds and
the ransack of hunters crackling the near branches.

She muttered, lifting her head a nod toward freedom,
I shall not, I shall not be moved.

She gathered her babies,
their tears slick as oil on black faces,
their young eyes canvassing mornings of madness.
Momma, is Master going to sell you
from us tomorrow?

Yes.
Unless you keep walking more
and talking less.
Yes.
Unless the keeper of our lives
releases me from all commandments.
Yes.
And your lives,
never mine to live,
will be executed upon the killing floor of innocents.
Unless you match my heart and words,
saying with me,

I shall not be moved.

In Virginia tobacco fields,
leaning into the curve

of Steinway
pianos, along Arkansas roads,
in the red hills of Georgia,
into the palms of her chained hands, she
cried against calamity,
You have tried to destroy me
and though I perish daily,

I shall not be moved.

Her universe, often
summarized into one black body
falling finally from the tree to her feet,
made her cry each time in a new voice,
All my past hastens to defeat,
and strangers claim the glory of my love,
Iniquity has bound me to his bed,

yet, I must not be moved.

She heard the names,
swirling ribbons in the wind of history:
nigger, nigger bitch, heifer,
mammy, property, creature, ape, baboon,
whore, hot tail, thing, it.
She said, But my description cannot
fit your tongue, for
I have a certain way of being in this world,

and I shall not, I shall not be moved.

No angel stretched protecting wings
above the heads of her children,
fluttering and urging the winds of reason

into the confusion of their lives.
They sprouted like young weeds,
but she could not shield their growth
from the grinding blades of ignorance, nor
shape them into symbolic topiaries.
She sent them away,
underground, overland, in coaches and
shoeless.
When you learn, teach.
When you get, give.
As for me,

I shall not be moved.

She stood in midocean, seeking dry land.
She searched God's face.
Assured,
she placed her fire of service
on the altar, and though
clothed in the finery of faith,
when she appeared at the temple door,
no sign welcomed
Black Grandmother. Enter here.

Into the crashing sound,
into wickedness, she cried,
No one, no, nor no one million
ones dare deny me God. I go forth
alone, and stand as ten thousand.

The Divine upon my right
impels me to pull forever
at the latch on Freedom's gate.

The Holy Spirit upon my left leads my
feet without ceasing into the camp of the
righteous and into the tents of the free.
These momma faces, lemon-yellow, plum-purple,
honey-brown, have grimaced and twisted
down a pyramid of years.
She is Sheba and Sojourner,
      Harriet and Zora,
      Mary Bethune and Angela,
      Annie to Zenobia.

She stands
before the abortion clinic,
confounded by the lack of choices.
In the Welfare line,
reduced to the pity of handouts.
Ordained in the pulpit, shielded
by the mysteries.
In the operating room,
husbanding life.
In the choir loft,
holding God in her throat.
On lonely street corners,
hawking her body.
In the classroom, loving the
children to understanding.

Centered on the world's stage,
she sings to her loves and beloveds,
to her foes and detractors:
However I am perceived and deceived,
however my ignorance and conceits,
lay aside your fears that I will be undone,

for I shall not be moved.

Preacher, Don't Send Me

Preacher, don't send me
when I die
to some big ghetto
in the sky
where rats eat cats
of the leopard type
and Sunday brunch
is grits and tripe.

I've known those rats
I've seen them kill
and grits I've had
would make a hill,
or maybe a mountain,
so what I need
from you on Sunday
is a different creed.

Preacher, please don't
promise me
streets of gold
and milk for free.
I stopped all milk
at four years old
and once I'm dead
I won't need gold.

I'd call a place
pure paradise

where families are loyal
and strangers are nice,

where the music is jazz
and the season is fall.
Promise me that
or nothing at all.

Fightin' Was Natural

Fightin' was natural,
hurtin' was real,
and the leather like lead
on the end of my arm
was a ticket to ride
to the top of the hill.
      Fightin' was real.

The sting of the ointment
and scream of the crowd
for blood in the ring,
and the clangin' bell cuttin'
clean through the
cloud in my ears.
      Boxin' was real.

The rope at my back
and the pad on the floor,
the smack of four hammers,
new bones in my jaw,
the guard in my mouth,
my tongue startin' to swell.
Fightin' was livin'.
Boxin' was real.
Fightin' was real.
      Livin' was . . . hell.

Loss of Love

The loss of love and youth
and fire came raiding,
riding,
a horde of plunderers
on one caparisoned steed,
sucking up the sun drops,
trampling the green shoots
of my carefully planted years.

The evidence: thickened waist and
leathery thighs, which triumph
over my fallen insouciance.

After fifty-five
the arena has changed.
I must enlist new warriors.
My resistance,
once natural as raised voices,
importunes in the dark.
Is this battle worth the candle?
Is this war worth the wage?

May I not greet age
without a grouse, allowing
the truly young to own
the stage?

Seven Women's Blessed Assurance

1

One thing about me,
I'm little and low,
find me a man
wherever I go.

2

They call me string bean
'cause I'm so tall.
Men see me,
they ready to fall.

3

I'm young as morning
and fresh as dew.
Everybody loves me
and so do you.

4

I'm fat as butter
and sweet as cake.
Men start to tremble
each time I shake.

5

I'm little and lean,
sweet to the bone.
They like to pick me up
and carry me home.

6

When I passed forty
I dropped pretense,
'cause men like women
who got some sense.

7

Fifty-five is perfect,
so is fifty-nine,
'cause every man needs
to rest sometime.

In My Missouri

In my Missouri
I had known a mean man
A hard man
A cold man
Gutting me and killing me
Was an Ice man
A tough man
A man.

So I thought I'd never meet a sweet man
A kind man
A true man
One who in darkness you can feel secure man
A sure man
A man.

But Jackson, Mississippi, has some fine men
Some strong men
Some black men
Walking like an army were the sweet men
The brown men
The men.

In Oberlin, Ohio, there were nice men
Just men
And fair men
Reaching out and healing were the warm men
Were good men
The men.

Now I know that there are good and bad men
Some true men

Some rough men
Women, keep on searching for your own man
The best man
For you man
The man.

They Ask Why

A certain person wondered why
a big strong girl like me
wouldn't keep a job
which paid a normal salary.
I took my time to lead her
and to read her every page.
Even minimal people
can't survive on minimal wage.

A certain person wondered why
I wait all week for you.
I didn't have the words
to describe just what you do.
I said you had the motion
of the ocean in your walk,
and when you solve my riddles
you don't even have to talk.

When Great Trees Fall

When great trees fall,
rocks on distant hills shudder,
lions hunker down
in tall grasses,
and even elephants
lumber after safety.

When great trees fall
in forests,
small things recoil into silence,
their senses
eroded beyond fear.

When great souls die,
the air around us becomes
light, rare, sterile.
We breathe, briefly.
Our eyes, briefly,
see with
a hurtful clarity.
Our memory, suddenly sharpened,
examines,
gnaws on kind words
unsaid,
promised walks
never taken.

Great souls die and
our reality, bound to
them, takes leave of us.
Our souls,
dependent upon their

nurture,
now shrink, wizened.
Our minds, formed
and informed by their
radiance,
fall away.
We are not so much maddened
as reduced to the unutterable ignorance
of dark, cold
caves.

And when great souls die,
after a period peace blooms,
slowly and always
irregularly. Spaces fill
with a kind of
soothing electric vibration.
Our senses, restored, never
to be the same, whisper to us.
They existed. They existed.
We can be. Be and be
better. For they existed.

ON THE
PULSE OF
MORNING

A Rock, A River, A Tree
Hosts to species long since departed,
Marked the mastodon,
The dinosaur, who left dried tokens
Of their sojourn here
On our planet floor,
Any broad alarm of their hastening doom
Is lost in the gloom of dust and ages.

But today, the Rock cries out to us, clearly, forcefully,
Come, you may stand upon my
Back and face your distant destiny,
But seek no haven in my shadow,
I will give you no hiding place down here.

You, created only a little lower than
The angels, have crouched too long in
The bruising darkness
Have lain too long
Facedown in ignorance,
Your mouths spilling words
Armed for slaughter.

The Rock cries out to us today,
You may stand upon me,
But do not hide your face.

Across the wall of the world,
A River sings a beautiful song. It says,
Come, rest here by my side.

Each of you, a bordered country,
Delicate and strangely made proud,
Yet thrusting perpetually under siege.

Your armed struggles for profit
Have left collars of waste upon
My shore, currents of debris upon my breast.
Yet today I call you to my riverside,
If you will study war no more.

Come, clad in peace,
And I will sing the songs
The Creator gave to me when I and the
Tree and the Rock were one.
Before cynicism was a bloody sear across your brow
And when you yet knew you still knew nothing.
The River sang and sings on.

There is a true yearning to respond to
The singing River and the wise Rock.
So say the Asian, the Hispanic, the Jew,
The African, the Native American, the Sioux,
The Catholic, the Muslim, the French, the Greek,
The Irish, the Rabbi, the Priest, the Sheik,
The Gay, the Straight, the Preacher,
The privileged, the homeless, the Teacher.
They hear. They all hear
The speaking of the Tree.

They hear the first and last of every Tree
Speak to humankind today.
Come to me,
Here beside the River.
Plant yourself beside the River.

Each of you, descendant of some passed-
On traveler, has been paid for.
You, who gave me my first name, you,

Pawnee, Apache, Seneca, you,
Cherokee Nation, who rested with me, then
Forced on bloody feet,
Left me to the employment of
Other seekers—desperate for gain,
Starving for gold.

You, the Turk, the Arab, the Swede,
The German, the Eskimo, the Scot,
The Italian, the Hungarian, the Pole,
You the Ashanti, the Yoruba, the Kru, bought,
Sold, stolen, arriving on a nightmare,
Praying for a dream.

Here, root yourselves beside me.
I am that Tree planted by the River,
Which will not be moved.
I, the Rock, I, the River, I, the Tree,
I am yours—your passages have been paid.
Lift up your faces, you have a piercing need
For this bright morning dawning for you.
History, despite its wrenching pain,
Cannot be unlived, but if faced
With courage, need not be lived again.

Lift up your eyes
Upon this day breaking for you.
Give birth again
To the dream.

Women, children, men,
Take it into the palms of your hands,
Mold it into the shape of your most
Private need. Sculpt it into

The image of your most public self.
Lift up your hearts.
Each new hour holds new chances
For a new beginning.
Do not be wedded forever
To fear, yoked eternally
To brutishness.

The horizon leans forward,
Offering you space
To place new steps of change.
Here, on the pulse of this fine day,
You may have the courage
To look up and out and upon me,
The Rock, the River, the Tree, your country.
No less to Midas than the mendicant.
No less to you now than the mastodon then.

Here, on the pulse of this new day,
You may have the grace to look up and out
And into your sister's eyes,
And into your brother's face,
Your country,
And say simply
Very simply
With hope—
Good morning.

CELEBRATIONS

A Brave and Startling Truth

DEDICATED TO THE HOPE FOR PEACE, WHICH LIES,
SOMETIMES HIDDEN, IN EVERY HEART.

We, this people, on a small and lonely planet
Traveling through casual space
Past aloof stars, across the way of indifferent suns
To a destination where all signs tell us
It is possible and imperative that we learn
A brave and startling truth.

And when we come to it
To the day of peacemaking
When we release our fingers
From fists of hostility
When we come to it
When the curtain falls on the minstrel show of hate
And faces sooted with scorn are scrubbed clean
When battlefields and coliseum
No longer rake our unique and particular sons and daughters
Up with the bruised and bloody grass
To lay them in identical plots in foreign soil

When the rapacious storming of the churches
The screaming racket in the temples have ceased
When the pennants are waving gaily
When the banners of the world tremble
Stoutly in a good, clean breeze

When we come to it
When we let the rifles fall from our shoulders
And our children can dress their dolls in flags of truce
When land mines of death have been removed

And the aged can walk into evenings of peace
When religious ritual is not perfumed
By the incense of burning flesh
And childhood dreams are not kicked awake
By nightmares of sexual abuse

When we come to it
Then we will confess that not the Pyramids
With their stones set in mysterious perfection
Nor the Gardens of Babylon
Hanging as eternal beauty
In our collective memory
Not the Grand Canyon
Kindled into delicious color
By Western sunsets

Nor the Danube, flowing its blue soul into Europe
Not the sacred peak of Mount Fuji
Stretching to the Rising Sun
Neither Father Amazon nor Mother Mississippi
who, without favor,
Nurtures all creatures in their depths and on their shores
These are not the only wonders of the world

When we come to it
We, this people, on this minuscule globe
Who reach daily for the bomb, the blade, and the dagger
Yet who petition in the dark for tokens of peace
We, this people, on this mote of matter
In whose mouths abide cankerous words
Which challenge our very existence

Yet out of those same mouths
Can come songs of such exquisite sweetness
That the heart falters in its labor
And the body is quieted into awe

We, this people, on this small and drifting planet
Whose hands can strike with such abandon
That, in a twinkling, life is sapped from the living
Yet those same hands can touch with such healing,
 irresistible tenderness,
That the haughty neck is happy to bow
And the proud back is glad to bend
Out of such chaos, of such contradiction
We learn that we are neither devils nor divines

When we come to it
We, this people, on this wayward, floating body
Created on this earth, of this earth
Have the power to fashion for this earth
A climate where every man and every woman
Can live freely without sanctimonious piety
Without crippling fear

When we come to it
We must confess that we are the possible
We are the miraculous, we are the true wonder of this world
That is when, and only when,
We come to it.

Continue

ON THE OCCASION OF OPRAH WINFREY'S
FIFTIETH BIRTHDAY

Dear Oprah,

On the day of your birth
The Creator filled countless storehouses and stockings
With rich ointments
Luscious tapestries
And antique coins of incredible value
Jewels worthy of a queen's dowry
They were set aside for your use
Alone

Armed with faith and hope
And without knowing of the wealth which awaited
You broke through dense walls
Of poverty
And loosed the chains of ignorance which
   threatened to cripple you so that you
   could walk
A free woman
Into a world which needed you

My wish for you
Is that you continue

Continue

To be who and how you are
To astonish a mean world
With your acts of kindness

Continue

To allow humor to lighten the burden
Of your tender heart

Continue

In a society dark with cruelty
To let the people hear the grandeur
Of God in the peals of your laughter

Continue

To let your eloquence
Elevate the people to heights
They had only imagined

Continue

To remind the people that
Each is as good as the other
And that no one is beneath
Nor above you

Continue

To remember your own young years
And look with favor upon the lost
And the least and the lonely

Continue

To put the mantle of your protection
Around the bodies of
The young and defenseless

Continue

To take the hand of the despised
And diseased and walk proudly with them
In the high street
Some might see you and
Be encouraged to do likewise

Continue

To plant a public kiss of concern
On the cheek of the sick
And the aged and infirm
And count that as a
Natural action to be expected

Continue

To let gratitude be the pillow
Upon which you kneel to
Say your nightly prayer
And let faith be the bridge
You build to overcome evil
And welcome good

Continue

To ignore no vision
Which comes to enlarge your range
And increase your spirit

Continue

To dare to love deeply
And risk everything
For the good thing

Continue

To float
Happily in the sea of infinite substance
Which set aside riches for you
Before you had a name

Continue

And by doing so
You and your work
Will be able to continue
      Eternally
          HAPPY BIRTHDAY!

Sons and Daughters

WRITTEN FOR THE CHILDREN'S
DEFENSE FUND

If my luck is bad
And his aim is straight
I will leave my life
On the killing field
You can see me die
On the nightly news
As you settle down
To your evening meal.

But you'll turn your back
As you often do
Yet I am your sons
And your daughters too.
In the city streets
Where the neon lights
Turn my skin from black
To electric blue
My hope soaks red
On the gray pavement
And my dreams die hard
For my life is through.

But you'll turn your back
As you often do
Yet I am your sons
And your daughters too.

In the little towns
Of this mighty land

Where you close your eyes
To my crying need
I strike out wild
And my brother falls
Turn on your news
You can watch us bleed.

In morgues I'm known
By a numbered tag
In clinics and jails
And junkyards too
You deny my kin
Though I bear your name
For I am a part
Of mankind too.

But you'll turn your back
As you often do
Yet I am your sons
And your daughters too.

Turn your face to me
Please
Let your eyes seek my eyes
Lay your hand upon my arm
Touch me. I am real as flesh
And solid as bone.

I am no metaphor
I am no symbol
I am not a nightmare
To vanish with the dawn
I am lasting as hunger
And certain as midnight.

I claim that no council nor committee
Can contain me
Nor fashion me to its whim.
You, come here, hunch with me in this dingy doorway,
Face with me the twisted mouth threat
Of one more desperate
And better armed than I.

Join me again at today's dime store counter
Where the word to me
Is still no.
Let us go, your shoulder,
Against my shoulder,
To the new picket line
Where my color is still a signal
For brutes to spew their bile
Like spit in my eye.

You, only you, who have made me
Who share this tender taunting history with me
My fathers and mothers
Only you can save me
Only you can order the tides,
That rush my heart, to cease
Stop expanding my veins
Into red riverlets.

Come, you my relative
Walk the forest floor with me
Where rampaging animals lurk,
Lusting for my future
Only if your side is by my side
Only if your side is by my side
Will I survive.

But you'll probably turn your back
As you often do
Yet I am your sons
And your daughters too.

A Black Woman Speaks to Black Manhood

READ BY THE POET AT THE MILLION MAN MARCH
IN WASHINGTON, D.C., ON OCTOBER 16, 1995

Our souls look back
In wondrous surprise
At how we have made it
So far from where we started

Fathers, brothers, uncles
Nephews, sons, and friends
Look over your shoulders
And at our history

The night was long
The wounds were deep
The pit has been dark
Its walls were steep

I was dragged by braids
On a sandy beach
I was pulled near you
But beyond your reach

You were bound and gagged
When you heard me cry
Your spirit was wounded
With each wrenching try

For you thrusted and pulled
Trying to break free
So that neither of us
Would know slavery

You forgot the strength
Of the rope and the chain
You only remember
Your manhood shame

You couldn't help yourself
And you couldn't help me
You've carried that fact
Down our history

We have survived
Those centuries of hate
And we do not deny
Their bruising weight

Please my many million men
Let us lay that image aside
See how our people today
Walk in strength and in pride

Celebrate, stand up, clap hands for ourselves and those who went
    before
Stand up, clap hands, let us welcome kind words back into our
    vocabulary
Stand up, clap hands, let us welcome courtesies back into our
    bedrooms
Stand up, clap hands, let us invite generosity back into our
    kitchens
Clap hands, let faith find a place in our souls
Clap hands, let hope live in our hearts
We have survived
And even thrived with
Passion
Compassion

Humor
and style

The night was long
The wounds were deep
The pit was dark
Its walls were steep

Clap hands, celebrate
We deserve it
Jubilate!

Amazing Peace

READ BY THE POET AT THE LIGHTING OF THE
NATIONAL CHRISTMAS TREE, WASHINGTON, D.C.,
DECEMBER 1, 2005

Thunder rumbles in the mountain passes
And lightning rattles the eaves of our houses.
Floodwaters await in our avenues.

Snow falls upon snow, falls upon snow to avalanche
Over unprotected villages.
The sky slips low and gray and threatening.

We question ourselves. What have we done to so affront nature?
We interrogate and worry God.
Are you there? Are you there, really?
Does the covenant you made with us still hold?

Into this climate of fear and apprehension, Christmas enters,
Streaming lights of joy, ringing bells of hope
And singing carols of forgiveness high up in the bright air.
The world is encouraged to come away from rancor,
Come the way of friendship.

It is the Glad Season.
Thunder ebbs to silence and lightning sleeps quietly in the corner.
Floodwaters recede into memory.
Snow becomes a yielding cushion to aid us
As we make our way to higher ground.

Hope is born again in the faces of children.
It rides on the shoulders of our aged as they walk into their sunsets.
Hope spreads around the earth, brightening all things,
Even hate, which crouches breeding in dark corridors.

In our joy, we think we hear a whisper.
At first it is too soft. Then only half heard.
We listen carefully as it gathers strength.
We hear a sweetness.
The word is Peace.
It is loud now.
Louder than the explosion of bombs.

We tremble at the sound. We are thrilled by its presence.
It is that for which we have hungered.
Not just the absence of war. But true Peace.
A harmony of spirit, a comfort of courtesies.
Security for our beloveds and their beloveds.

We clap hands and welcome the Peace of Christmas.
We beckon this good season to wait awhile with us.
We, Baptist and Buddhist, Methodist and Muslim, say come.
Peace.
Come and fill us and our world with your majesty.
We, the Jew and the Jainist, the Catholic and the Confucian,
Implore you to stay awhile with us
So we may learn by your shimmering light
How to look beyond complexion and see community.

It is Christmas time, a halting of hate time.

On this platform of peace, we can create a language
To translate ourselves to ourselves and to each other.

At this Holy Instant, we celebrate the Birth of Jesus Christ
Into the great religions of the world.
We jubilate the precious advent of trust.
We shout with glorious tongues the coming of hope.

All the earth's tribes loosen their voices
To celebrate the promise of Peace.

We, Angels and Mortals, Believers and Nonbelievers,
Look heavenward and speak the word aloud.
Peace. We look at our world and speak the word aloud.
Peace. We look at each other, then into ourselves,
And we say without shyness or apology or hesitation:

Peace, My Brother.
Peace, My Sister.
Peace, My Soul.

Mother

A CRADLE TO HOLD ME

It is true
I was created in you.
It is also true
That you were created for me.
I owned your voice.
It was shaped and tuned to soothe me.
Your arms were molded
Into a cradle to hold me, to rock me.
The scent of your body was the air
Perfumed for me to breathe.

Mother,
During those early, dearest days
I did not dream that you had
A larger life which included me,
Among your other concerns,
For I had a life
Which was only you.

Time passed steadily and drew us apart.
I was unwilling.
I feared if I let you go
You would leave me eternally.
You smiled at my fears, saying
I could not stay in your lap forever
That one day you would have to stand

And where would I be?
You smiled again.
I did not.

Without warning you left me,
But you returned immediately.
You left again and returned,
I admit, quickly.
But relief did not rest with me easily.
You left again, but again returned.
You left again, but again returned.
Each time you reentered my world
You brought assurance.
Slowly I gained confidence.

You thought you knew me,
But I did know you,
You thought you were watching me,
But I did hold you securely in my sight,
Recording every movement,
Memorizing your smiles, tracing your frowns.
In your absence
I rehearsed you,
The way you had of singing
On a breeze,
While a sob lay
At the root of your song.

The way you posed your head
So that the light could caress your face
When you put your fingers on my hand
And your hand on my arm,
I was blessed with a sense of health,
Of strength and very good fortune.

You were always
The heart of happiness to me,

Bringing nougats of glee,
Sweets of open laughter.

I loved you even during the years
When you knew nothing
And I knew everything, I loved you still.
Condescendingly of course,
From my high perch
Of teenage wisdom.
I spoke sharply to you, often
Because you were slow to understand.
I grew older and
Was stunned to find
How much knowledge you had gleaned.
And so quickly.

Mother, I have learned enough now
To know I have learned nearly nothing.
On this day
When mothers are being honored,
Let me thank you
That my selfishness, ignorance, and mockery
Did not bring you to
Discard me like a broken doll
Which had lost its favor.
I thank you that
You still find something in me
To cherish, to admire, and to love.

I thank you, Mother.
I love you.

In and Out of Time

FOR JESSICA AND COLIN JOHNSON
STEPHANIE AND GUY JOHNSON

The sun has come out
The mists have gone
We see in the distance
Our long way home

I was yours to love
You were always mine
We have belonged together
In and out of time

When the first stone looked
Up at the blazing sun
And the first tree struggled
From the forest floor
I loved you more

You were the rhythm on the head
Of the conga drum
And the brush of palm
On my nut brown skin

And I loved you then

We worked the cane
And cotton fields
We trod together
The city streets

Wearied by labor
Bruised by cruelty
Strutting and sassy
To our inner beat

And all the while
Lord, how I love your smile

You've freed your braids
Gave your hair to the breeze
It hummed like a hive
Of busy bees
I reached into the mass
For the honeycomb there
God, how I loved your hair

You saw me bludgeoned
By circumstance
Injured by hate
And lost to chance
Legs that could be broken
But knees that would not bend
Oh, you loved me then

I raked the Heavens' belly
With torrid screams
I fought to turn
Nightmares into dreams
My protests were loud
And brash and bold
My, how you loved my soul

The sun has come out
The mists have gone
We see in the distance
Our long way home

I was yours to love
And you were always mine
We have belonged together
In and out of time

Ben Lear's Bar Mitzvah

AN ODE TO BEN LEAR ON THE
OCCASION OF HIS BAR MITZVAH

To you
in your walled city of childhood,
the years have inched by slowly, tortoise-like crawling,
yet to your family and family of friends
the time has hurried, without halting,
without leaving enough seasons in which
to know you, to teach you, to love you.
You have been noted studying the Torah,
probing the words of ancient prophets reading,

To many
you have come too suddenly to the new region of manhood.

To your parents,
in whose immense realm of love
you have been clasped and claimed,
you are still the tender-tough boy,
yet in your face, they see already the promise of the man you
　　are becoming.
To them
you are too eager to step into the new land,
too ready to share the responsibility
with the citizens of your new country.
Some of your beloveds
are longing to hold you back in the safe arms of childhood,
where errant behavior could meet with soft admonishment,
where most injuries could be made better by a mother's kiss,
but even now you are leaning away toward the horizon

with one foot raised to step forward.
None can stop you, none can stay you.

Please know,
prayers lay in the road where you will plant your feet.
Please know
that aspirations of your family are high at your back, and surround
    you entirely.
Please know
that great hopes of your devoted shower you with
ardent wishes for your being and for your future.
Your beloveds
know that you are entering a nation
where you must learn the difference
between seeking after justice
and lusting for revenge.
They know also
that you will meet those who would be kind
if only they had the courage, and
those who would do evil
if only they had the opportunity.
You will be bathed in the morning dew of truth
and you will drink down the brackish water of false witness.
Be wary, my nephew, but fear only God,
for you have a limitless resource of powerful love
to evoke and call forth
and I,
prompt with all your primed and loving family,
await your summons.

Vigil

FOR LUTHER VANDROSS AND BARRY WHITE

We are born in pain, then relief comes.
We are lost in the dark, then day breaks.
We are confused, confounded, and fearful,
Then faith takes our hand.
We stumble and fumble and fall,
Then, we rise.

Into each of our meanest nights, you have arrived,
Oh, Lord,
Creator,
To lead us away from our ignorance
And into knowing.

Now, we gather at your altar,
Rich and poor, young and
Achingly old,
We are the housed and the homeless,
We are the lucky,
And the lazy.

As if at the foot
Of an ancient baobab tree,
In this moment
We gather to stand, kneel, sit, squat, and crumple here,
Knowing that, when the medical geniuses
Have done their best,
When the Nobel Prize Winners
Have used their most powerful energy,
We have You.

Creator,
We bring to You
Our brothers, sons, fathers, uncles,
Nephews, cousins, beloved, and friends.

We place the body of Luther Vandross
And the body of Barry White
Here before You.
They are among the best we have
And You are all we have.

Heal, we pray.

Heal, we pray.

Heal us all,

We pray.

Prayer

Father Mother God, thank You for Your presence during the hard
and mean days. For then we have You to lean upon.

Thank You for Your presence during the bright and sunny days, for
then we can share that which we have with those who have less.

And thank You for Your presence during the Holy Days, for then
we are able to celebrate You and our families and our friends.

For those who have no voice, we ask You to speak.

For those who feel unworthy, we ask You to pour Your love out in
waterfalls of tenderness.

For those who live in pain, we ask You to bathe them in the river of
Your healing.

For those who are lonely, we ask You to keep them company.

For those who are depressed, we ask You to shower upon them the
light of hope.

Dear Creator, You, the borderless sea of substance, we ask You to
give to all the world that which we need most—Peace.

Amen.

AMAZEMENT
AWAITS

Sheer amazement awaits
Amazement luxuriant in promise
Abundant in wonder
Our beautiful children arrive at this Universal stadium.

They have bathed in the waters of the world
And carry the soft silt of the Amazon, the Nile,
The Danube, the Rhine, the Yangtze and the Mississippi
In the palms of their right hands.
A wild tiger nestles in each armpit
And a meadowlark perches on each shoulder.

We, the world audience, stand, arms akimbo,
Longing for the passion of the animal:
The melody of the lark
And the tigers' passion
Attend the opening bells,
The birds sing of the amazement which awaits.

The miracle of joy that comes out of the gathering of our best,
    bringing their best,
Displaying the splendor of their bodies and the radiance of their
    agile minds to the cosmos.
Encouragement to those other youth caught in the maws of poverty,
Crippled by the terror of ignorance.

They say,
Brothers and Sisters,
Yes, try.
Then try harder.

Lunge forward, press eagerly for release.
The amazement which awaits is for you.

We are here at the portal of the world we had wished for
At the lintel of the world we most need.
We are here roaring and singing.
We prove that we can not only make peace, we can bring it with us.

With respect for the world and its people,
We can compete passionately without hatred.
With respect for the world and its people,
We can take pride in the achievement of strangers.
With respect for the world and its people,
We can share openly in the success of friends.

Here then is the Amazement:
Against the odds of impending war,
In the mouth of bloody greed,
Human grace and human spirit can still conquer.

Ah . . .
We discover, we ourselves
Are the Amazement which awaits
We are ourselves Amazement.

HIS DAY

IS

DONE

TO ALL THE
WORLD'S CITIZENS,
WHO LOST A FRIEND
WHEN PRESIDENT
NELSON MANDELA
DIED

Education is the most powerful weapon
you can use to change the world.

—NELSON MANDELA

His day is done,
Is done.

The news came on the wings of a wind
Reluctant to carry its burden.

Nelson Mandela's day is done.

The news, expected and still unwelcome,
Reached us in the United States and suddenly

Our world became somber.
Our skies were leadened.

His day is done.

We see you, South African people,
Standing speechless at the slamming
Of that final door
Through which no traveler returns.

Our spirits reach out to you:
Bantu, Zulu, Xhosa, Boer.

We think of you
And your Son of Africa,
Your Father,
Your One More Wonder of the World.

We send our souls to you
As you reflect upon
Your David armed with
A mere stone facing down
The Mighty Goliath.

Your man of strength, Gideon,
Emerging triumphant
Although born into the brutal embrace of Apartheid,
Scarred by the savage atmosphere of racism,
Unjustly imprisoned
In the bloody maws of South African dungeons.

Would the man survive?
Could the man survive?

His answer strengthened men and women
Around the world.

In the Alamo in San Antonio, Texas,
On the Golden Gate Bridge in San Francisco,
In Chicago's Loop,
In New Orleans' Mardi Gras,
In New York City's Times Square,
We watched as the hope of Africa sprang
Through the prison's doors.

His stupendous heart intact,
His gargantuan will
Hale and hearty.

He had not been crippled by brutes
Nor was his passion for the rights

Of human beings
Diminished by twenty-seven years of imprisonment.

Even here in America
We felt the cool
Refreshing breeze of freedom
When Nelson Mandela took
The seat of the presidency
In his country
Where formerly he was not even allowed to vote.
We were enlarged by tears of pride
As we saw Nelson Mandela's
Former prison guards
Invited, courteously, by him to watch
From the front rows
His inauguration.

We saw him accept
The world's award in Norway
With the grace and gratitude
Of Solon in Ancient Grecian courts
And the confidence of African Chiefs
From ancient royal stools.

No sun outlasts its sunset
But will rise again
And bring the dawn.

Yes, Mandela's day is done,

Yet we, his inheritors,
Will open the gates wider
For reconciliation.

And we will respond
Generously to the cries
Of the Blacks and Whites,
Asians, Hispanics,
The poor who live piteously
On the floor of our planet.

He has offered us understanding.
We will not withhold forgiveness
Even from those who do not ask.

Nelson Mandela's day is done.

We confess it in tearful voices
Yet we lift our own to say:

Thank You.

Thank You, Our Gideon.
Thank You, Our David.
Our great courageous man.

We will not forget you.
We will not dishonor you.
We will remember and be glad

That you lived among us

That you taught us
And
That you loved us
All!

MAYA ANGELOU was raised in Stamps, Arkansas. In addition to her bestselling autobiographies, including *I Know Why the Caged Bird Sings* and *The Heart of a Woman*, she wrote numerous volumes of poetry, among them *Phenomenal Woman, And Still I Rise, On the Pulse of Morning*, and *Mother*. Maya Angelou died in 2014.

This book was set in Requiem, a typeface designed by the Hoefler Type Foundry. It is a modern typeface inspired by inscriptional capitals in Ludovico Vicentino degli Arrighi's 1523 writing manual, *Il modo de temperare le penne.* An original lowercase, a set of figures, and an italic in the chancery style that Arrighi (fl. 1522) helped popularize were created to make this adaptation of a classical design into a complete font family.